Guided Math Lessons in Second Grade

Guided Math Lessons in Second Grade provides detailed lessons to help you bring guided math groups to life. Based on the bestselling *Guided Math in Action*, this practical book offers 16 lessons, taught in a round of 3—concrete, pictorial, and abstract. The lessons are based on the priority standards and cover fluency, word problems, operations and algebraic thinking, and place value. Author Dr. Nicki Newton shows you the content as well as the practices and processes that should be worked on in the lessons, so that students not only learn the content but also how to solve problems, reason, communicate their thinking, model, use tools, use precise language, and see structure and patterns.

Throughout the book, you'll find tools, templates, and blackline masters so that you can instantly adapt the lesson to your specific needs and use it right away. With the easy-to-follow plans in this book, students can work more effectively in small guided math groups—and have loads of fun along the way!

Dr. Nicki Newton has been an educator for over 30 years, working both nationally and internationally with students of all ages. She has worked on developing Math Workshop and Guided Math Institutes around the country; visit her website at www.drnickinewton.com. She is also an avid blogger (www.guidedmath.wordpress.com), tweeter (@drnickimath) and Pinterest pinner (www.pinterest.com/drnicki7).

Also Available from Dr. Nicki Newton

(www.routledge.com/eyeoneducation)

Guided Math Lessons in First Grade:
Getting Started

Guided Math Lessons in Kindergarten:
Getting Started

Day-by-Day Math Thinking Routines in Kindergarten:
40 Weeks of Quick Prompts and Activities

Day-by-Day Math Thinking Routines in First Grade:
40 Weeks of Quick Prompts and Activities

Day-by-Day Math Thinking Routines in Second Grade:
40 Weeks of Quick Prompts and Activities

Day-by-Day Math Thinking Routines in Third Grade:
40 Weeks of Quick Prompts and Activities

Day-by-Day Math Thinking Routines in Fourth Grade:
40 Weeks of Quick Prompts and Activities

Day-by-Day Math Thinking Routines in Fifth Grade:
40 Weeks of Quick Prompts and Activities

Leveling Math Workstations in Grades K–2:
Strategies for Differentiated Practice

Daily Math Thinking Routines in Action:
Distributed Practices Across the Year

Mathematizing Your School:
Creating a Culture for Math Success
Co-authored by Janet Nuzzie

Math Problem Solving in Action:
Getting Students to Love Word Problems, Grades K–2

Math Problem Solving in Action:
Getting Students to Love Word Problems, Grades 3–5

Guided Math in Action:
Building Each Student's Mathematical Proficiency With Small-Group Instruction

Math Workshop in Action:
Strategies for Grades K–5

Math Running Records in Action:
A Framework for Assessing Basic Fact Fluency in Grades K–5

Math Workstations in Action:
Powerful Possibilities for Engaged Learning in Grades 3–5

Guided Math Lessons in Second Grade

Getting Started

Dr. Nicki Newton

Routledge
Taylor & Francis Group

NEW YORK AND LONDON

First published 2022
by Routledge
605 Third Avenue, New York, NY 10158

and by Routledge
2 Park Square, Milton Park, Abingdon, Oxon, OX14 4RN

Routledge is an imprint of the Taylor & Francis Group, an informa business

Library of Congress Cataloging-in-Publication Data
Names: Newton, Nicki, author.
Title: Guided math lessons in second grade : getting started / Dr. Nicki Newton.
Description: New York, NY : Routledge, 2021.
Identifiers: LCCN 2021001717 (print) | LCCN 2021001718 (ebook) | ISBN
    9780367901929 (hardback) | ISBN 9780367901912 (paperback) | ISBN
    9781003022954 (ebook)
Subjects: LCSH: Mathematics—Study and teaching (Elementary) | Group
    guidance in education. | Group work in education.
Classification: LCC QA20.G76 N52 2021 (print) | LCC QA20.G76 (ebook) |
    DDC 372.7/044—dc23
LC record available at https://lccn.loc.gov/2021001717
LC ebook record available at https://lccn.loc.gov/2021001718

ISBN: 978-0-367-90192-9 (hbk)
ISBN: 978-0-367-90191-2 (pbk)
ISBN: 978-1-003-02295-4 (ebk)

Typeset in Palatino
by Apex CoVantage, LLC

This series is dedicated to Lin Goodwin. She has been a magnificent part of my becoming a teacher educator. I worked under her tutelage for several years at Columbia University. She led me, guided me, and taught me a whole bunch of stuff about teaching and learning. She also chaired my dissertation committee. I will ever be grateful to her and I thank God for putting her in my life as one of my guiding angels.

Contents

Acknowledgments

I thank God for life and happiness. I thank my family and friends for all their support. I thank my editor Lauren who is the best in the world! I thank all the reviewers who gave feedback that helped make the series what it is! I thank the copyediting and production team for getting it to print.

I would also like to thank Math Learning Center (https:/www.mathlearningcenter.org/apps), Braining Camp (https://www.brainingcamp.com/) and Didax (https://www.didax.com/math/virtual-manipulatives.html) for the use of screenshots of their fabulous virtual manipulatives.

I also would like to thank Pixabay for great pictures: https://pixabay.com/

Meet the Author

Dr. Nicki Newton has been an educator for over 30 years, working both nationally and internationally, with students of all ages. Having spent the first part of her career as a literacy and social studies specialist, she built on those frameworks to inform her math work. She believes that math is intricately intertwined with reading, writing, listening, and speaking. She has worked on developing Math Workshop and guided math institutes around the country. Most recently, she has been helping districts and schools nationwide to integrate their state standards for mathematics and think deeply about how to teach these within a Math Workshop model. Dr. Nicki works with teachers, coaches, and administrators to make math come alive by considering the powerful impact of building a community of mathematicians who make meaning of real math together. When students do real math, they learn it. They own it, they understand it, and they can do it. Every one of them. Dr. Nicki is also an avid blogger (www.guidedmath.wordpress. com), tweeter (drnickimath) and Pinterest pinner (www.pinterest.com/drnicki7/).

Dr. Nicki Newton, Educational Consultant
Phone: 347–688–4927
Email: drnicki7@gmail.com

Find More Online!

Resources, videos, and conversations with Dr. Nicki can be found the Guided Math Dropbox Resources: https://bit.ly/2Ja4sMY

1

Introduction

Figure 1.1 Guided Math Example 1

I pull a group of second graders who are working on their make 10 facts. This particular group of students is still really shaky on making 10, so we are using the ten frame and playing a game where they have to build the number and then say how many more to 10. It provides them with a scaffold (which will eventually be phased out). They giggle with a sense of confidence as they pull and show the fact. When we are done, we talk about what we did and students give examples. They also talk about who thinks this is easy and who thinks it is tricky.

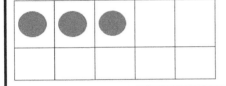

Figure 1.2 Guided Math Example 2

I pull a different group of second graders and we are working on doubles plus 1 facts. They all are quite proficient in doubles. They have moved on to a different strategy. We are playing a doubles domino game. They have to pull a double plus 1 domino and calculate the sum. Whoever has the largest sum wins a counter. Whoever gets 10 counters first wins the game. They have a toolbox right there in case they need a number path, rekenrek, or ten frame. Some of them just know it while others are counting on using their fingers.

Guided math is a small-group instructional strategy that teaches students in their zone of proximal development around the priority standards. There are so many standards, but every state has priority focus standards. Those are the standards that you teach in a small guided math group. It is a time for hands-on, minds-on learning based on the standards. It is a time for discussing ideas, listening to the thinking of others, reasoning out loud, and becoming a confident, competent mathematician.

Guided math groups are for everyone! Too often, students are rushed through big ideas, understandings, and skills. They are left with ever widening gaps. Guided math groups give teachers the time needed to work with students in a way that they can all learn. Guided math groups can be used to remediate, to teach on grade-level concepts, and to address the needs of students that are working beyond grade level.

Guided math groups can be heterogeneous or homogeneous. It depends on what you are trying to do. If you are teaching a specific skill, counting on, one group could be working with visually leveled flashcards and another group could be working with more abstract number

Figure 1.3 Visually Leveled Flashcards   **Figure 1.4** Marked Number Line

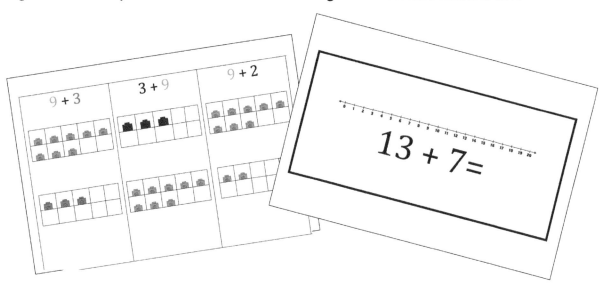

flashcards. You could also pull a group that is still exploring it just concretely on the beaded number line for another session. The groups are flexible, and students work in different groups at different times, never attached to any one group for the entire year. Students meet in a particular guided math group for three or four times based on their specific instructional needs and then they move on.

Guided math groups can occur in all types of classrooms. Typically, they are part of a Math Workshop. In a Math Workshop (see Figure 1.5) there are three parts.

Opening

♦ Energizers and Routines
♦ Problem Solving
♦ Mini-Lesson

Student Activity

♦ Math Workstations
♦ Guided Math Groups

Debrief

♦ Discussion
♦ Exit Slip
♦ Mathematician's Chair Share

What Are the Other Kids Doing?

The other students should be engaged in some type of independent practice. They can be working alone, with partners, or in small groups. They could be rotating through stations based on a designated schedule or they could be working from a menu of Must Do's and Can Do's. The point is that students should be practicing fluency, word problems, place value, and working on items in the current unit of study. This work should be organized in a way that students are working in their zone of proximal development (Vygotsky, 1978).

Differentiating workstations helps to purposefully plan for the learning of all students. The fluency workstation games should be divided by strategy, for example students can be working on either make 10 facts, doubles, or bridge 10 facts, depending on what they need (Baroody, 2006; Van de Walle, 2007; Henry & Brown, 2008). Another example is word problems. There are 15 single step problems that second graders are exposed to. Knowing the learning trajectory and understanding the structures that go from simple to complex can help organize the teaching and learning of word problems (Carpenter, Fennema, Franke, Levi, & Empson, 1999/2015; Fuchs et al., 2010; Jitendra, Hoff, & Beck, 1999).

Figure 1.5

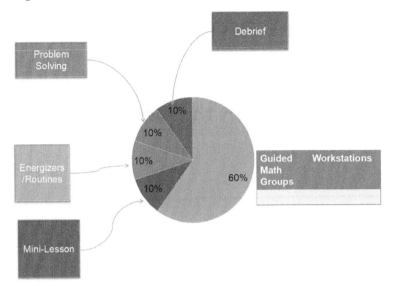

Figure 1.6 Workstations 1

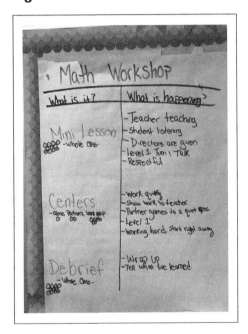

Figure 1.7 Workstations 2

Benefits of Guided Math Groups

♦ See student knowledge in action.
♦ Monitor the concepts and skills that are understood.
♦ Catch and address the misunderstandings.
♦ Ask questions that highlight thinking.
♦ Analyze thinking.
♦ Listen to conversations.
♦ Assess in the moment.
♦ Redirect in the moment.
♦ Differentiate as needed.

Workstation Contract

I have the privilege of learning with the Math Workstations.

I will play fair.

I will be a good sport. When I win, I will celebrate appropriately. When I lose, I'll be a good sport.

I will use the math manipulatives the way they are supposed to be used.

I will use the digital resources the way they are supposed to be used.

I will put everything back neatly.

I will work hard every day.

I will keep trying when the going gets tough!

My Signature:_____

Date: _____

Key Points

◆ Different Reasons: remediate, focus on grade-level topics or working beyond grade level
◆ Cycle of Engagement: concrete, pictorial, abstract
◆ Heterogeneous and Homogeneous Grouping
◆ Math Workshop
◆ Math Workstations
◆ Benefits of Guided Math

Summary

Guided math is a great way to differentiate learning for all your students. Focus on the priority standards. Students approach these standards through a concrete, pictorial, and abstract cycle of engagement. Sometimes, the groups are homogeneous groups and other times the groups are heterogeneous. Guided math groups can be done in a variety of ways, either traditional setups or a Math Workshop model. The other students should always be doing work that they are familiar with and are practicing in the math workstation. Many times, the work that students are working on in the guided math group is carried over into the math workstation. When the students are in guided math groups, the other students should be meaningfully engaged in math workstations. All of this works together to give all students a chance to learn.

Reflection Questions

1. How are you differentiating instruction around the priority standards right now?
2. Currently, how do you group students? What informs your grouping?
3. Do you have a plan to make sure that everybody fully understands the priority standards?

References

Baroody, A. J. (2006). Why children have difficulties mastering the basic number combinations and how to help them. *Teaching Children Mathematics, 13*, 22–32.

Carpenter, T. P., Fennema, E., Franke, M. L., Levi, L., & Empson, S. B. (1999/2015). *Children's mathematics: Cognitively guided instruction.* Portsmouth, NH: Heinemann.

Fuchs, L., Zumeta, R., Schumacher, R., Powell, Seethaler, O., Hamlett, C., & Fuchs, D. (2010). The effects of schema-broadening instruction on second graders' word-problem performance and their ability to represent word problems with algebraic equations: A randomized control study. *Elementary School Journal, 110*(4), 446–463. Retrieved January 4, 2020, from www.ncbi.nlm.nih.gov/pubmed/20539822

Henry, V. J., & Brown, R. S. (2008). First-grade basic facts: An investigation into teaching and learning of an accelerated, high-demand memorization standard. *Journal for Research in Mathematics Education*, 153–183.

Jitendra, A. K., Hoff, K., & Beck, M. M. (1999). Teaching middle school students with learning disabilities to solve word problems using a schema based approach. *Remedial and Special Education, 20*, 50–64.

Van de Walle, J. (2007). *Elementary and middle school mathematics: Teaching developmentally.* Boston: Pearson/Allyn and Bacon.

Vygotsky, L. S. (1978). *Mind in society: The development of higher psychological processes.* Cambridge, MA: Harvard University Press.

2
Behind the Scenes

Assessment

Assessment is a crucial element in designing a guided a math lesson. Teachers have to know where their students are along the trajectory of learning so that they can plan to teach them purposefully. Teachers need actionable data. Actionable data is data that can be used immediately to develop meaningful lessons. At the beginning of the year, teachers need to get data about the priority standards/major cluster standards from the year before so they can figure out if there are any gaps and make a plan to close them. Richardson (n.d.) notes, "The information gathered from the assessments helps teachers pinpoint what each child knows and still needs to learn. They are not about 'helping children be right,' but about uncovering their instructional needs."

Math running records are a great way to check fluency! It's the GPS of fact fluency.

Remember, every summer students lose at least 2.6 months of math (Shafer, 2016). Teachers should assess fluency, word problems, operations and algebraic thinking, and place value in the beginning of the year. At the middle of the year, teachers should assess all the grade-level work done in these areas during the first part of the year. At the end of the year, teachers should assess all the priority standards for the grade. Throughout the year, teachers should rely on entrance and exit slips (Figure 2.2), quizzes, anecdotals, unit assessments, and conferences to get information about students.

Grouping

Guided math groups should have between three and five students. Sometimes they are heterogeneous groups and sometimes they are homogeneous groups. It depends on what you are trying to do. If you are working on big ideas and understanding, you might pull a small group of students and have them work on modeling with different tools. You might pull students together and work on some word problems. However, if you are working on adding basic facts and on a specific strategy, you might pull a group that is working on making 10. You might pull another group that you work with using the doubles facts. You can also pull groups by their choice or interest. Groups should last between 10 and 15 minutes. Remember the attention span rule: age plus a few minutes.

Differentiation

After teachers get the data, they need to use it to differentiate (see Figure 2.1). Some of the work is to close the gaps. Some of the work is to accelerate the learning of the advanced students. Some of the work is to teach in the grade-level zone. A big part of the differentiation aspect of guided math lessons is the concrete, pictorial, and abstract cycle. Sometimes, students know the answer but do not necessarily understand the math. It is crucial to do quick assessments with students to make sure that they understand the math. For example, a student might know

Figure 2.1 Math Running Records Example

Addition Running Record Recording Sheet

Student: _____ Teacher: _____ Date: _____

Part 1	Codes: What do you notice?	Initial Observations of Strategies	Data Code Names
0 + 1 a 5s pth	ca fco cah coh wo sc asc dk	0 1 2 3 4M 4	A0----- add 0
2 + 1 a 5s pth	ca fco cah coh wo sc asc dk	0 1 2 3 4M 4	A1----- add 1
3 + 2 a 5s pth	ca fco cah coh wo sc asc dk	0 1 2 3 4M 4	Aw5--- add w/in 5
2 + 6 a 5s pth	ca fco cah coh wo sc asc dk	0 1 2 3 4M 4	Aw10—add w/in 10
4 + 6 a 5s pth	ca fco cah coh wo sc asc dk	0 1 2 3 4M 4	AM10---add making 10
10 + 4 a 5s pth	ca fco cah coh wo sc asc dk	0 1 2 3 4M 4	A10-----add 10 to a #
7 + 7 a 5s pth	ca fco cah coh wo sc asc dk	0 1 2 3 4M 4	AD------add doubles
5 + 6 a 5s pth	ca fco cah coh wo sc asc dk	0 1 2 3 4M 4	AD1-----add dbls +/-1
7 + 5 a 5s pth	ca fco cah coh wo sc asc dk	0 1 2 3 4M 4	AD2----add dbls +/-2
9 + 6 a 5s pth	ca fco cah coh wo sc asc dk	0 1 2 3 4M 4	AHF/C9-add higher facts use compensation w/9
8 + 4 a 5s pth	ca fco cah coh wo sc asc dk	0 1 2 3 4M 4	AHF/C7/8—add higher facts/use compensation with 7/8
7 + 8 a 5s pth	ca fco cah coh wo sc asc dk	0 1 2 3 4M 4	AHF/C7/8—add higher facts/use compensation with 7/8

Codes	Types of Strategies	Strategy Levels	
a - automatic 5s - 5 seconds pth - prolonged thinking time	ca - counted all fco – finger counted on cah – counted all in head coh – counted on in head wo - wrong operation sc - self corrected asc - attempted to self-correct dk - didn't know	0 – doesn't know 1 – counting strategies by ones or skip counting using fingers, drawings or manipulatives 2 - mental math/solving in head 3 - using known facts and strategies 4M - automatic recall from memory 4 – automatic recall and students have number sense	

(Continued)

(Continued)

Part 2: Flexibility/Efficiency			
Teacher: We are now going to administer Part 2 of the Running Record. In this part of the Running Record we are going to talk about what strategies you use when you are solving basic addition facts. I am going to tell you a problem and then ask you to tell me how you think about it. I am also going to ask you about some different types of facts. Take your time as you answer and tell me what you are thinking as you see and do the math. I am going to take notes so I can remember everything that happened during this Running Record.			
Add 0 0 + 1 What happens when you add zero to a number? ___ same # ___other ___can't articulate What would be the answer to... 3 + 0 0 + 5 8 + 0 Do they know this strategy? No/Emerging/Yes A0 Level 0 1 2 3 4M 4	**Add 1 2 + 1** What strategy do you use when you add 1 to a number? ___ next counting # ___other ___can't articulate What would be the answer to.... 4 + 1 1 + 7 10 + 1 Do they know this strategy? No/Emerging/Yes A1 Level 0 1 2 3 4M 4	**Add w/in 5 or 10 3 + 2 2 + 6** How do you solve 4 + 0? And 6 + 3? ___ count on from big # __ other ___can't articulate w/in 5 w/in 10 1 + 3 5 + 4 2 + 2 2 + 7 Do they know this strategy? No/Emerging/Yes A10 Level 0 1 2 3 4M 4	**Add to Make 10 4 + 6** How do you solve 5 + 5? ___ count on from big # __ other ___can't articulate I'm going to give you a number and I want you to give me the number that makes 10 with it. If I give you 7, how many more to make 10? If I give you ____ how many more to 10? 9? 2? 6? 3? Do they know this strategy? No/Emerging/Yes AM10 Level 0 1 2 3 4M 4
Add 10 10 + 4 What strategy do you use when you add 10 to a number? ___ teen #s decompose to 10 and 1's ____other ___can't articulate How would you solve ____? 10 + 2 10 + 6 10 + 8 Do they know this strategy? No/Emerging/Yes A10 Level 0 1 2 3 4M 4	**Doubles 7 + 7** How would you solve 6 + 6? ___ doubles ___ other ___can't articulate How would you solve _____? 4 + 4 8 + 8 9 + 9 What kind of facts are these? _____ Do they know this strategy? No/Emerging/Yes AD Level 0 1 2 3 4M 4	**Doubles +/- 1 5 + 6** How would you solve 6 + 7? ___ doubles +/-1 ___ other ___can't articulate How would you solve ____? 2 + 3 3 + 4 8 + 9 Do they know this strategy? No/Emerging/Yes AD1 Level 0 1 2 3 4M 4	**Doubles +/- 2 7 + 5** If a friend did not know how to solve 7 + 9, what would you tell her to do? ___ doubles +/-2 ___other ___can't articulate How would you solve....? 2 + 4 8 + 6 9 + 11 Do they know this strategy? No/Emerging/Yes AD2 Level 0 1 2 3 4M 4

Bridge through 10 (9) 9 + 6	Bridge through 10 (7/8) 8 + 4	Part 3: Mathematical Disposition
If your friend was stuck solving 9 + 5, what would you tell him to do? ___ bridge 10 ___other ___can't articulate	What strategy would you use to solve 8 + 3? ___ bridge 10 ___other ___can't articulate	Do you like math? What do you find easy? What do you find tricky? What do you do when you get stuck?
How do you solve _____? 9 + 3 9 + 6 Do they know this strategy? No/Emerging/Yes AHF/C9 Level 0 1 2 3 4M 4	How would you solve ____? 4 + 7? 8 + 5? Do they know this strategy? No/Emerging/Yes AHF/C 7/8 Level 0 1 2 3 4M 4	Question Prompts: That's interesting/fascinating: tell me what you did. That's interesting/fascinating: tell me how you solved it. That's interesting/fascinating: tell me what you were thinking. How did you solve this problem? Can you tell me more about how you solve these types of problems? What do you mean when you say _____? (i.e. ten friends/neighbor numbers etc.)

General Observations (to be filled out after the interview)

Instructional Response:
Fluency Focus areas (circle all that apply): flexibility   efficiency   accuracy   automaticity

What addition strategy should the instruction focus on?

A0 A1 Aw5 Aw10 AM10 A10 AD AD1 AD2 AHF/C9 AHF/C 7/8

For his/her current instructional level, what is the predominant way in which the student is arriving at the answers? 0 1 2 3 4M 4 _____

Overall, what is the way in which the students calculated the answers?: 0 1 2 3 4M 4

Comments/Notes about gestures, behaviors, remarks:

*In most states k fluency is within 5 and 1st grade fluency is within 10 and 2nd grade within 20. However, some states k is within 10 and 1st and 2nd is within 20.

Figure 2.2 Exit Slip Example

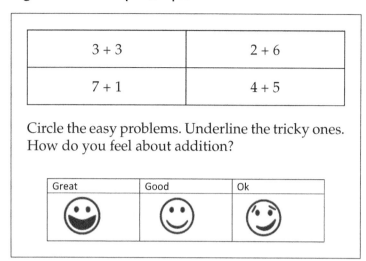

3 + 3	2 + 6
7 + 1	4 + 5

Circle the easy problems. Underline the tricky ones. How do you feel about addition?

Great	Good	Ok
😀	🙂	🙂

that 6 + 5 is 11 by counting up. So, they can get an answer but they don't have strategic competence. We want them to have flexibility with numbers, thinking 6 + 5 is 5 plus 5 plus 1 more, or 6 + 6 − 1, or another efficient strategy. We would practice it in a variety of ways with manipulatives, with sketches, and with the numbers. We would also have the students verbalize what they are doing and contextualize it by telling stories (NCTM, 2014).

Figure 2.3 Differentiation

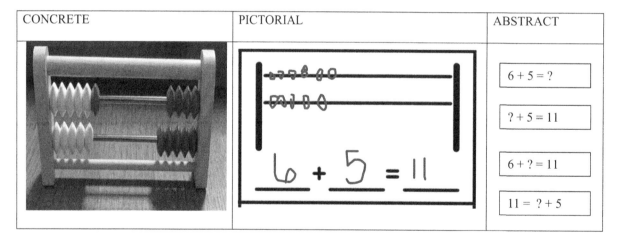

CONCRETE	PICTORIAL	ABSTRACT
	6 + 5 = 11	6 + 5 = ? ? + 5 = 11 6 + ? = 11 11 = ? + 5

Types of Groups

When we are thinking about grouping, it is about meeting the needs of the students where they are and taking them to what they need to learn at that grade level. So students are emerging in their learning along the continuum. It is about creating flexible groups that students can move through as they work on different concepts. These groups should never be "fixed" or track students throughout the year. They are temporary, flexible, focused groups that teach students what they need, when they need it and then students move on to different work.

Figure 2.4 Types of Groups

Group 1: Emergent	Group 2: Early Fluent	Group 3: Fluent	Group 4: Advanced Fluent
These are the students that are working below grade level. They often have many gaps and misunderstandings. It is important to work on closing gaps as well as highly scaffolding (but not overscaffolding) current grade-level material.	These students are approaching grade level. They have some gaps and need some remediation.	These students are right at grade level.	These students are working above grade level. This doesn't mean that the work should be done from the next grade level though; as Kathy Richardson notes, it is important to go deeper with concepts rather than to jump to the next ones.
A student can be an emergent learner in one area and an advanced fluent learner in another. These are not meant to be labels that stick with students all year. As Dr. Kim Reid always said, "Labels are for boxes" (personal communication). Although we need a way to describe how students are doing in particular areas, we must never categorize them with fixed labels. Students move and develop along their own trajectory. With the appropriate scaffolding, we can teach everybody and move them to achieving grade-level standards. Rather than viewing some children as "low" or "behind" or "lacking in skills," kidwatching teachers view all children as creative, capable learners – on their way to "achieving control over the conventions of [math]- always 'in process' always moving forward..." (Flukey, 1997 p.219 cited in Owocki & Goodman, 2002)." Students move and develop along their own trajectory. With the appropriate scaffolding we can teach everybody and move them to achieving grade level standards and beyond.			

Rotations

Teachers can assign students where they are going to go, visiting different stations every day. Another way to do it is to give the student a menu for the week with can do's and must do's. Either way, students should do fluency, word problems, place value, and work from the current unit of study.

Standards-Based

Every guided math lesson should be centered on priority standards. There are so many standards to teach, so we have to focus. We have to get in there, dig deep, and discuss ideas so that students can learn them. When students sit down in the group, the first thing the teacher should talk about is the work they are going to be doing for the day. The "I can" or "I am learning to" statement should be up and the students should discuss what they are going to be learning and what the criteria of success for that learning will look like. There is an ongoing discussion about whether to say "I can" or "I am learning to." "I can" is more of a statement about what students will be able to do in the future. "I am learning to" speaks more to the continuum of learning and allows for students to be at different places along that continuum.

Dixon points out that, sometimes, we shouldn't always tell the students the I can statement at the beginning because then in essence you tell the ending of the story before it begins (2018a). This is an excellent point; it depends on where you are at in the concept and skill cycle and what the lesson of the day is. If you are trying to get students to explore and wonder about something, then don't upfront it, but discuss it at the end after they have explored the topic. However, if you are working on something that you have been doing for a while, you can say, "Today we are going to continue looking at . . ."

Depth of Knowledge

Guided math lessons are about building depth of knowledge (DOK) with students. They should reach a variety of levels, not just level 1 activities. For example, instead of just telling stories such as "There were 5 ducks and 2 more came. How many ducks are there?" teachers should ask questions such as "The answer is 5 ducks. What is the question?" Instead of just asking what 3 + 2 is, teachers should also say things like "Give me two different ways to make 5." We want students to reason about numbers in a variety of ways, using as many scaffolds as they need to become confident and competent.

Scaffolding

Scaffolds are a fundamental part of guided math lessons. There are so many different types of scaffolds. We are going to discuss grouping scaffolds, language scaffolds, and tool scaffolds. Grouping scaffolds help students become proficient by having them work with partners and in small groups, before they practice the skill on their own. This is the social aspect of grappling with the content. Oftentimes, students learn a great deal from each other through discussions and interactions. In the group, you can partner the students up and watch them play the game and take notes and ask different questions to guide them as they work together.

Language is often scaffolded with illustrated pictures of the vocabulary and language stems on sentence strips. Dixon (2018b) discusses how in the beginning of learning about a concept, it can be productive for students to have to explain the topic without the "cover" of the vocabulary. Meaning that sometimes students will use words but not understand the concepts, and their lack of understanding can be hidden by the use of the correct vocabulary. If they don't have that, then they have to explain the math. In later lessons, when students understand the math, then it's ok to upfront the vocabulary.

Scaffolding is so important, yet we have to be really careful not to overscaffold and, as Dixon warns, to also avoid "just in case" scaffolding (2018c). We want to help students as they need it, but we do not want to steal the struggle. Students need the opportunity to engage in the productive struggle, but it should not be an unproductive struggle (Hiebert & Grouws, 2007; Blackburn, 2018). There is a very careful balancing act that teachers conduct when scaffolding in a guided math group.

In the guided math group, teachers should make sure that tools are part of the learning cycle. In planning to unpack the concepts and skills in small groups, teachers should think about the ways in which students can wrestle with topics concretely, pictorially, and abstractly. They should also emphasize verbalization and contextualization (NCTM, 2014). The magic of the manipulatives is the conversation and the activities that are done along with them. Students need to reflect on and explain the concepts and how the manipulatives are being used to model those concepts. In a small group, students should be doing the math and exploring and discussing the ideas as they use the manipulatives (Ball, 1992; Baroody, 1989; Bruner, 1960; Burns, n.d.)

Engagement

Engagement is important. Research links engagement to students' *affect*—their feelings and emotions about learning (McLeod, 1992, cited in Ingram). We find that students' engagement is shaped around the sociocultural environment in which they are learning, how they are constructing knowledge together through discussions, activities, and the norms of learning (Op 't Eynde, 2004; Boaler & Greeno, 2000; Greeno, Collins, & Resnick, 1996). The interactions that students have in small guided math groups are very important. They help to shape students' mathematical identities—who and what they see themselves as in terms of being a mathematician.

We find that students are engaged when they participate in strong lessons in a strong community. A strong lesson has a clear purpose, is relevant, and makes sense to their lives; it is brain-friendly and flows easily, allowing them to quickly get into a "good 'workflow'" and dive deep into the material (Claflin, 2014). A strong community of learners in essence means that "they've got each other's back!" Everybody is in it to win it with each other. Students are helpful, trusting, risk-taking, and comfortable. In the small group, they should be willing to try things out and be assured that it is not always going to work the first time and they might not get it even the second time around, but that with perseverance they can learn it.

Another really important aspect of working with small children is the wonder of learning. The guided math table is a special experience. I like to have guided math journals and special pencils and toolkits for students to work with at the table. Students look forward to coming to the guided math group. Often, I use dice, dominos, cards, and board games. Since the same structure can be used, the students are ready to work on the content. Meaning, if we play bingo, then students know that structure, so they can immediately focus on the content. I might play a doubles bingo game with one group and a make 10 bingo game with another group.

Student Accountability

While the students are working in math workstations, they should be filling out different sheets of the work they are doing (see Figures 2.5, 2.6, and 2.7). They should be recording what they are doing. Some sheets record everything that students are doing. Other games have students record only some of their work.

The most important thing about Math Workshop is that you organize it well from the beginning. You must do the first 20 days. In the first 20 days you teach the students how to work in the workshop. Here is a resource for that: www.drnickinewton.com/downloads/

Students have to learn how to work independently before you start pulling them into guided math groups. The premise of Math Workshop is to let all students work on their own productively, before you start working with them in small groups.

There are two key elements to a good workstation. The first is a clear goal for the workstation. Students need to know what the math is, how they are going to work on that math, and what it looks like when they are actually learning that math. The second is that they have an accountability system so that they know the teacher will be monitoring their work.

Figure 2.5 Student Recording Sheet Example 1

Comparing Numbers		
Roll the dice. Record your roll. Compare with the symbols. Whoever has the highest number wins a point. Whoever gets 5 points first wins the round. Whoever wins 3 rounds wins the game.		
Partner 1	**< = >**	**Partner 2**

Figure 2.6 Student Recording Sheet Example 2

Recording Sheet: Top It
I had 7 + 8 which made 15. My partner had 4 + 5 which made 9. I had more because 15 is greater than 9.

1	2	3	4	5	6	7	8	9	10	11	12	13	14	15	16	17	18	19	20

_____ is greater than _____.

_____ is less than _____.

_____ is the same as _____.

Figure 2.7 Student Recording Sheet Example 3

Recording Sheet: Board Game

When I went around the board I solved several half facts problems. I can use my doubles to help me.

I solved:

$14 - 7 = 7$
$12 - 6 = 6$
$10 - 5 = 5$

Key Points

♦ Assessment
♦ Grouping
♦ Differentiation
♦ Rotations
♦ Standards-Based
♦ Depth of Knowledge
♦ Scaffolding
♦ Engagement
♦ Student Accountability

Summary

The key to great guided math groups is assessment. When you have great assessments, you can group appropriately for differentiation that matters. Lessons should be standards-based. Teachers must always plan for the level of rigor in the lesson. Lessons should be scaffolded with language supports, tools, templates, and student grouping. All the other students must be accountable for the work they are doing in the workstations. Engagement is necessary.

Reflection Questions

1. What specific assessments do you have around the priority standards?
2. In what ways are you evaluating your lessons for rigor?
3. In what ways are you scaffolding lessons?
4. How do you know that the other students are on task and learning in the math workstation?

References

Ball, D. L. (1992). Magical hopes: Manipulatives and the reform of math education. *American Educator: The Professional Journal of the American Federation of Teachers, 16*(2), 14–18, 46–47.

Baroody, A. J. (1989). Manipulatives don't come with guarantees. *Arithmetic Teacher, 37*(2), 4–5.

Blackburn, B. (2018). Retrieved January 5, 2020, from www.ascd.org/ascd-express/vol14/num11/productive-struggle-is-a-learners-sweet-spot.aspx

Boaler, J., & Greeno, J. G. (2000). Identity, agency, and knowing in mathematical worlds. In J. Boaler (Ed.), *Multiple perspectives on mathematics teaching and learning* (pp. 171–200). Westport, CT: Ablex Publishing.

Bruner, J. S. (1960). On learning mathematics. *The Mathematics Teacher, 53*(8), 610–619.

Burns, M. (n.d.). *How to make the most of manipulatives.* Retrieved August 28, 2016, from http://teacher.scholastic.com/lessonrepro/lessonplans/instructor/burns.htm?nt_id=4&url=http://store.scholastic.com/Books/Hardcovers/Harry-Potter-and-the-Chamber-of-SecretsThe-Illustrated-Edition-Book-2?eml=SSO/aff/20160429/21181/banner/EE/affiliate/////2-247765/&affiliate_id=21181&click_id=1707726852

Claflin, P. (2014). Retrieved January 20, 2020, from www.theanswerisyes.org/2014/12/08/student-engagement-checklist/

Dixon. (2018a). Retrieved January 4, 2020, from www.dnamath.com/blog-post/five-ways-we-undermine-efforts-to-increase-student-achievement-and-what-to-do-about-it/

Dixon. (2018b). Retrieved January 4, 2020, from www.dnamath.com/blog-post/five-ways-we-undermine-efforts-to-increase-student-achievement-and-what-to-do-about-it-part-4-of-5/

Dixon. (2018c). Retrieved January 4, 2020, from www.dnamath.com/blog-post/five-ways-we-undermine-efforts-to-increase-student-achievement-and-what-to-do-about-it-part-3-of-5/
Greeno, J. G., Collins, A. M., & Resnick, L. B. (1996). Cognition and learning. In D. C. Berliner & R. C. Calfee (Eds.), *Handbook of educational psychology* (pp. 15–46). London: Prentice Hall International.

Hiebert, J., & Grouws, D. A. (2007). The effects of classroom mathematics teaching on students' learning. In F. K. Lester (Ed.), *Second handbook of research on mathematics teaching and learning* (pp. 371–404). Charlotte, NC: Information Age.

McLeod, D. B. (1992). Research on affect in mathematics education: A reconceptualization. In D. Grouws (Ed.), *Handbook of research on mathematics teaching and learning* (pp. 575–596). New York: NCTM, Palgrave Macmillan.

National Council of Teachers of Mathematics. (2014). *Principles to actions: Ensuring mathematical success for all.* Reston, VA: Author.

Op 't Eynde, P. (2004). A socio-constructivist perspective on the study of affect in mathematics education. In M. J. Hoines & A. B. Fuglestad (Eds.), *28th conference of the international group for the psychology of mathematics education* (Vol. 1, pp. 118–122). Bergen, Norway: Bergen University College.

Owocki, G., & Goodman, Y. M. (2002). Kidwatching: Documenting children's literacy development. Portsmouth, NH: Heinemann.

Richardson, K. (n.d.). Retrieved January 17, 2020, from http://assessingmathconcepts.com/

Shafer, L. (2016). *Summer math loss: Why kids lose math knowledge, and how families can work to counteract it.* Retrieved January 15, 2019, from www.gse.harvard.edu/news/uk/16/06/summer-math-loss

3
Architecture of a Small-Group Lesson

Guided math groups can appear as many different things. Sometimes they are more of an exploration of a concept with manipulatives like ten frames and counters, other times they are skill practice in the form of a dice game. The elements of the guided math lesson are the same, but the sequencing can be different. For example, you might start with an energizer and then review a skill and play a game to practice that skill. On the other hand, you might be exploring decompositions of a number with Cuisenaire™ rods first and then afterwards discuss what the math you were exploring was about.

Every small-group lesson should begin with an introduction to the lesson. In this introduction, students will often go over the agenda. The teacher should usually write it up as an agenda so students know what the general outline of the lesson is and what they will be doing. At some point in the lesson, depending on the type of lesson, the teacher would then go over the "I am learning to" statement as well as what it looks like when students can actually do that skill or understand that concept.

After that is discussed, everyone should talk about the math vocabulary and phrases that are associated with the current topic, if they are already familiar with the words. This is very important because everyone will use this vocabulary throughout the lesson. However, sometimes the vocabulary is discussed at the end of the lesson (see Dixon, 2018). In this case, the students talk about what they were doing and name it with math words.

Then, the lesson begins with either a discussion, an exploration, or an activity. The teacher might model it or might just jump into the topic. Oftentimes, the teacher will ask the students to give their input about the topic before they begin. After a time of exploration, the students will begin to further explore the topic, either on their own, with a partner, or with the whole small group.

At the end, the teacher will lead the debrief. This is where the students will discuss what the math was for the day, as well as how they practiced that math. They should also talk about how they feel they are doing with that math. This is the part of the lesson where students are reflecting and monitoring their process. They talk about the parts of the topic that are "easy-peasy" and the parts that are "tricky." Language is important, so instead of saying difficult or hard, I tend to say "tricky, fuzzy, or climbing." Using a mountain metaphor can help students explain their journey. I explain to students that they could be just looking at the mountain from the base, climbing but not at the top yet, almost at the top, or at the top (whereby they can say, "it's sunny on the summit").

Planning

Planning is key (see Figures 3.1 through 3.6 for templates). As you are planning for the guided math lesson, it is important to think about the differences between the content, the context, and the activity. The content could be to teach students how to compose ten. The context could be a story about finding ways to make 10. The activity could be to play a card game where they have to make 10s. This comes up when mapping math content. There is a difference between an activity and a skill. An activity is to actually do something, like play a doubles board game. The skill is the verb—to be able to double a number. The teacher should be planning success criteria for both the product and the process. An example of the content criteria:

I am going to *play a make 5 game.*
So that I can *practice make 5 facts.*
I will know that I can do it *when I can make 5 from any number from 0 to 5 using mental math.*

An example of process criteria is to think about what practices you want students to be able to do:

◆ I can *explain* how to make 5 with any number.
◆ I can *model* a make 5 fact.

Clarke states that when we define process success criteria for students, it helps them do these six things:

1. Ensure appropriate focus
2. Provide opportunity to clarify their understanding
3. Identify success for themselves
4. Begin to identify where the difficulties lie
5. Discuss how they will improve
6. Monitor their own progress

(cited in Dyer, n.d.)

In the guided math group, everyone should know what the criteria are and should discuss them. Dyer notes,

> When students are allowed to answer the question "How will we know?" and when they understand the learning behind the learning target, they are developing their own success criteria. This enables students to better understand what teachers expect them to know, understand, or be able to do, as well as what constitutes a proficient performance. This allows students to support each other and take responsibility for their own learning by helping them accurately and appropriately evaluate learning against shared expectations and make any necessary adjustments to the learning. Students become activated as learners.
>
> (n.d.)

Think about this in terms of your guided math lessons. Do the students understand the success criteria? Do they know what they are expected to know, understand, and be able to do? What are you looking for in the products or performances to know that the students were successful? How will you judge if it was successful? What will you use to judge the effectiveness of the product or performance? What counts as successful?

If the objective is for students to learn different efficient, flexible strategies for adding, then the success criteria might be:

◆ Students' explanations include the names of the strategies.
◆ Students can discuss different ways to think about the same problem.

- In the explanations, students include a clear description of what they did (they can verbalize the strategy).
- Students can model their thinking.

You could also have this discussion at the end of the lesson, after students have explored many different strategies. You could then talk about what it means to be flexible and efficient. You could have a checklist or rubric that has the criteria on it.

In the guided math group, the goal is for both teacher and students to be questioning. The expected answers should require thinking, not just a quick yes or no. Students should be thinking and explaining the work. Guided math should not be show and tell. It should be teachers spring boarding students into mathematical thinking. The guided math group is a space for the "having of very good ideas" by all. In the guided math group, the students should by taking the responsibility for learning and reflecting on their learning, as well as evaluating themselves and others. They should not be passive listeners or just "yes men and women." They should be active participants in the construction of rich mathematical ideas. To make this happen, there must be a great deal of planning.

More Planning

In the guided math group, there can be an agenda. Whether or not you make it public, the teacher should have an idea of the structure of the lesson. I usually make it public.

Introduction

Agenda

- I am learning to/I can
- Vocabulary/Language Frames
- Launch by Teacher
- Student Activity (alone/pairs/group)
- Wrap-Up/Reflection
- Next Steps

Planning and Preparation

Figure 3.1 Quick Plan

Week	Assessments	Workstations
Big Idea:	Entrance Slips:	Group 1
Enduring Understanding:	Exit Slips:	Group 2
Essential Question		Group 3
I am learning to . . .		Group 4

Figure 3.2 Guided Math Planning Template 1

	Group 1:	Group 2:	Group 3:	Group 4:
Unit of Study: **Big Idea:** **Enduring Understanding:** **Standard:**	**Essential Question:** **Vocabulary:** **Language Frame:** **I Can Statement:**			
Monday	Lesson: Materials: DOK Level: Concrete/Pictorial/ Abstract	Lesson: Materials: DOK Level: Concrete/Pictorial/ Abstract	Lesson: Materials: DOK Level: Concrete/Pictorial/ Abstract	Lesson: Materials: DOK Level: Concrete/Pictorial/ Abstract
Tuesday	Lesson: Materials: DOK Level: Concrete/Pictorial/ Abstract	Lesson: Materials: DOK Level: Concrete/Pictorial/ Abstract	Lesson: Materials: DOK Level: Concrete/Pictorial/ Abstract	Lesson: Materials: DOK Level: Concrete/Pictorial/ Abstract
Wednesday	Lesson: Materials: DOK Level: Concrete/Pictorial/ Abstract	Lesson: Materials: DOK Level: Concrete/Pictorial/ Abstract	Lesson: Materials: DOK Level: Concrete/Pictorial/ Abstract	Lesson: Materials: DOK Level: Concrete/Pictorial/ Abstract
Thursday	Lesson: Materials: DOK Level: Concrete/Pictorial/ Abstract	Lesson: Materials: DOK Level: Concrete/Pictorial/ Abstract	Lesson: Materials: DOK Level: Concrete/Pictorial/ Abstract	Lesson: Materials: DOK Level: Concrete/Pictorial/ Abstract
Friday	Lesson: Materials: DOK Level: Concrete/Pictorial/ Abstract	Lesson: Materials: DOK Level: Concrete/Pictorial/ Abstract	Lesson: Materials: DOK Level: Concrete/Pictorial/ Abstract	Lesson: Materials: DOK Level: Concrete/Pictorial/ Abstract

Figure 3.3 Guided Math Planning Template 2

Guided Math Groups	
Big Ideas: Enduring Understandings: Essential Questions: Vocabulary: Language Frames:	Cycle of Engagement: Concrete, Pictorial, Abstract Depth of Knowledge Level: 1 2 3 4 Standard/I can statement:
Group 1:	Group 2:
Group 3:	Group 4:

Figure 3.4 Guided Math Planning Template 3

Guided Math Lesson Plan: Group:		
Week: Big Idea: Enduring Understanding:	Standard: I can/I am learning to statement:	Vocabulary: Language Frame: Materials:
Lesson: Intro: Guided Practice: Individual Practice: Sharing: Debrief:		
Comments/Notes: Next Steps:		

Figure 3.5 Guided Math Planning Template 4

Guided Math Lesson		
Big Ideas: Enduring Understandings: Essential Questions:	Vocabulary: Language Frame:	Standard: I can/I am learning to . . . Concrete/Pictorial/Abstract
DOK Level: 1 2 3 4	Goal: ♦ Remediate ♦ Teach ♦ Dive Deeper	Materials/Tools _see table below_
Beginning of the Lesson	Guided Practice	Independent Practice
Assessment/Exit Slip	Discussion	Questions
Comments/Notes: Ahas: Wow: Rethink: Next Moves:		

Materials/Tools:

dice	board games	unifix cubes/bears/tiles
domino	counters	base ten blocks
deck of cards	calculators	pattern blocks
white boards/markers	gm journals	geoboards

Figure 3.6 Guided Math Planning Template 5

Guided Math		
Group: **Week:**		
Big Idea: Enduring Understandings: Essential Questions:	Vocabulary: Language Frame: DOK Level: 1 2 3 4	Lessons: 1st 2nd 3rd
Content Questions:		
Name	What I Noticed	Next Steps

Figure 3.7 Differentiated Lessons

Topic:	
Big Idea: **Enduring Understanding:** **Essential Question:** **I can statement:**	**Materials**
Cycle of Engagement **Concrete:** **Pictorial:** **Abstract:**	**Vocabulary & Language Frames** Vocabulary: Talk Frame:
	Other Notes:

Figure 3.8 Guided Math Planning Sheet

Three Differentiated Lessons		
Emerging	On Grade Level	Above Grade Level

WATCH OUT — Misunderstandings and Misconceptions

Figure 3.9 Key Points

Guided Math Planning Sheet	
Launch	
Model	
Checking for Understanding	
Guided Practice/ Checking for Understanding	
Set Up for Independent Practice	

Key Points

♦ Architecture of the Lesson

  ○ I am learning to/I can
  ○ Vocabulary/Language Frames
  ○ Launch by Teacher
  ○ Student Activity (alone/pairs/group)
  ○ Wrap-Up
  ○ Next Steps

♦ Planning Template
♦ Discussion Throughout

Summary

There is a suggested architecture for small guided math groups. Teachers must plan for the learning goal, the vocabulary supports, the tools, the launch of the lesson, the students practicing the math and the wrap-up, the reflection, and the next steps. All of these elements are an important part of the lesson. They all contribute to the success of the guided math group. Using planning templates, with these elements on them, helps teachers plan for each of the elements.

Reflection Questions

1. Do your guided math lessons have all of the elements in them?
2. What types of templates are you currently using for guided math groups?
3. What is an element that you need to focus on in the architecture?

References

Dixon, J. Small Group Instruction {from the (Un)Productive Practices Series}. Five Ways we Undermine Efforts to Increase Student Achievement (and what to do about it) Blog Post 4: http://www.dnamath.com/blog-post/five-ways-we-undermine-efforts-to-increase-student-achievement-and-what-to-do-about-it-part-4-of-5/

Dixon. (2018). Retrieved January 4, 2020, from www.dnamath.com/blog-post/five-ways-we-undermine-efforts-to-increase-student-achievement-and-what-to-do-about-it-part-4-of-5/

Dyer, K. (n.d.). Retrieved January 20, 2020, from www.nwea.org/blog/2018/what-you-need-to-know-when-establishing-success-criteria-in-the-classroom/

4

Guided Math Talk

One of the most important things that happens in the guided math group is the discussion. We have to teach students to be active participants and engaged listeners. We want them to respect each other deeply and seek to truly understand each other without judgement. They have to learn to develop and defend their thinking, justify their answers, and respectfully disagree with each other. The National Council of Teachers of Mathematics (NCTM) defines math talk as "the ways of representing, thinking, talking, and agreeing and disagreeing that teachers and students use to engage in [mathematical] tasks" (NCTM, 1991).

Questions

It is so important to ask good questions. The questions should reach beyond the answer. As Phil Daro notes, we have to go "beyond answer-getting." The questions in the guided math group should be designed to get students to understand more fundamentally the mathematics of the grade level. Good questions don't just happen—they are planned for. The teacher should know ahead of time the types of questions that she will ask and why she will ask them. In the plan for the lesson, the teacher should brainstorm some possible questions that push student thinking. These are not yes or no questions, but rather ones that require students to explain themselves, show what they know, and defend and justify their thinking (see Figure 4.1).

When students are sitting in that group, they should be having an engaging experience that builds mathematical knowledge and skills. At the table, students should be encouraged to actively participate. They should be thinking out loud, sharing their thoughts, respectively analyzing and critiquing the thoughts and actions of others, and taking risks throughout the explorations. We should always be thinking about the levels of rigor of the conversation that the students are engaged in (see Figure 4.2).

In terms of rigor, there are four levels of questions.

It is very important to include open questions as part of your repertoire at the guided math table. Here is an example: "The answer is 12 elephants. What is the question?"

Although you will ask some questions that require students to remember a fact or show you that they can do a skill, your questions must extend beyond this level. You should be focusing on questions that have more than one answer or way of solving the problem.

Questions That Pique Curiosity

Your questions should pique curiosity. They should lead students into further explorations. They don't have to be answered immediately. Students should have a sense of wonder. There should be some "Aha" moments, some "Wow" moments, and some "I don't get it" moments.

For example, "What if we didn't have addition?" "Tell me three situations in which you would use subtraction." "Why is addition important in real life?"

Figure 4.1 Planning for Great Questions

Before the Lesson	During the Lesson	After the Lesson
Plan what you want to get your students to think about. The tasks that we choose will determine the thinking that occurs.	**Observe, monitor, and note what is happening in the group. Checklists, post-its, and anecdotal note structures work well here.**	**Reflect, assess, and decide what's next.**
How will you go about that? What questions will you ask them?	What is your data collection system during the lesson?	What did you see?
		What did you hear?
How will you set them up to actively listen and productively participate?	How will you scaffold student questioning?	What did the students do?
How will you get them to engage with the ideas of others?	How will you scaffold student-to-student interactions?	What do you need to do next?
		What instructional moves will you make?
How will you get them to offer detailed explanations of their own thinking using numbers, words, and models?		What pedagogical moves will you make?
Plan for misconceptions. How will you address them and redirect students?		

Figure 4.2 Depth of Knowledge

DOK 1	DOK 2	DOK 3
	At this level, students explain their thinking.	At this level, students have to justify, defend, and prove their thinking with objects, drawings, and diagrams.
What is the answer to . . . ? Can you model the problem? Can you identify the answer that matches this equation?	How do you know that the equation is correct? Can you pick the correct answer and explain why it is correct? How can you model that problem in more than one way? What is another way to model that problem? Can you model that on the. . . ? Give me an example of a . . . type of problem . . . Which answer is incorrect? Explain your thinking.	Can you prove that your answer is correct? Prove that . . . Explain why that is the answer. . . . Show me how to solve that and explain what you are doing. Defend your thinking.

Note: Level 4 is more strategic project-based thinking.

Student-to-Student Conversations

It is crucial that the teacher sets up a discussion where students ask each other questions. They could have question rings, bookmarks, mini-anchor charts, or other scaffolds to help them ask each other questions (see Figures 4.3–4.5). In these conversations, one of the things that students are doing is listening to each other and comparing what they did.

Probing Questions

Teacher questions as well as student-to-student questions should provide insight into student thinking. During the guided math lesson and after it, the teacher should jot down what they have learned about student thinking, student knowledge, and how students are making sense of the math they are learning.

Figure 4.3 Question Bookmark

Question Bookmark
Questions we could ask each other.   How do you know?   Are you sure about that?   What is another way to do that?   Why did you use that model?   Can you explain your thinking?

Figure 4.4 Talk Cards/Talk Ring

I agree because...	I disagree because...	I need some time to think.	Why is that true?

Are you sure?	Do you agree or disagree?	Can you think of another way?	I'm confused still..
Yes, I'm sure because No, I'm not sure. I'm thinking about it.	or	Way 1 Way 2	

Figure 4.5 5 Talk Moves Poster

5 Talk Moves				
Revoice	Restate	Reason	Wait Time	Group participation
I heard you say...	*Who can say what she said in your own words?*	*Are you sure? Can you prove it?*	*Give me a few seconds*	*Who wants to add to that?*

Scaffolding Questions for ELLs

Students should understand the questions being asked. The language should be accessible, and everyone should have a way to enter into the conversation. When thinking about instruction with English language learners (ELLs), we must consider the type of language support they will need (https://mathsolutions.com/math-talk/; http://fspsscience.pbworks.com/w/file/fetch/80214878/Leveled_20Questions_20for_20ELLs; www.aworldoflanguagelearners.com/asking-answering-questions-with-ells/). Oftentimes, they will need help with syntax and sentence structure, so it is important to scaffold these into the conversation. Give students an opportunity to refer to language stems, use language bookmarks, and write down and/or draw the answer (see Figure 4.6).

Figure 4.6 Scaffolding for ELLs

Low levels of support: (advanced language learners) (levels 3 & 4)	Moderate levels of support: (developing language learners) (level 2)	High levels of support: (emerging language learners) (level 1)
Use a word bank (illustrated)	Use a sentence frame	Allow students to draw/ write the answer
Explain how s/he did that?	I got the answer by _____.	Point to the . . .
Explain your thinking?	How can you use ____ to help you solve _____?	Show me your answer. . . .
Explain your model/ strategy?	How can you model that?	Which is the best answer?
What are two ways you could model your thinking?	What is the name of that strategy? (mini-anchor chart)	What is the name of that strategy? Do you see it here? (mini-anchor chart of strategies)
Can you describe your thinking?	How did you do that?	
Can you show us what you did?	Why did you use that model/strategy?	Give students a model sentence and a sentence frame.
Can you describe how you did it?	How did s/he do that?	How did you get the answer?
	Is it this or that?	How did you _____?
Can you explain what s/he did?	Which strategy did you use? (visual support)	Do you agree? Yes or no
Why is that true?		Show me the _____.
Why is that not true?		Circle the ____.
Explain how you did it.		Can you point to the strategy you used?
Decide if s/he is correct.		

Although these are structures for ELLs, they are great question types to consider with the various students you are working with. They are also great ways to think about scaffolding questions for special education students.

Five Talk Moves and More

The idea of having a framework for how students engage with each other is very important. Chapin, O'Connor, and Anderson (2009) theorized this framework around five talk moves: revoicing, restating, wait time, group participation, and reasoning. There are also other really helpful frameworks (Kazemi & Hintz, 2014; O'Connell & O'Connor, 2007). In the following section, we will explore how some of these can help us structure the discussions in guided math groups. Oftentimes, these structures are used together, for example a teacher might ask someone to restate what someone said and then encourage the group to add on (see Figures 4.7 to 4.15).

Figure 4.7 Revoicing

What It Is	What It Does	What It Sounds Like
The teacher restates in the words of the student what they just said.	This allows the student to hear back what they said, the other students to hear and process what has been said, and everyone to think about it and make sure they understand it. This teaches students the power of hearing what they have said and trying to make sense of it.	*So you said . . . Is that correct?* *Let me make sure I understand, you are saying . . .* *So first you . . . and then you . . .* *So you used this model?* *So you used this strategy?*

Figure 4.8 Restating

What It Is	What It Does	What It Sounds Like
The teacher or other students restate in their own words what has been said. Then, they verify that restating with the original student.	This allows the student to hear back what they said, the other students to hear and process what has been said, and everyone to think about it and make sure they understand it. This requires that students listen and pay attention to each other so they can restate what has been said. This teaches students how to listen to each other and make sense of what their peers are saying.	*Who can restate what Susie just said?* *Who can tell in their own words what Jamal just said?* *Who can explain what Carol meant when she said. . . ?*

Figure 4.9 Reasoning

What It Is	What It Does	What It Sounds Like
Teachers and students are asking each other for evidence and proof to defend and justify what they are saying.	This requires students to engage with each other's thinking. They must compare, contrast, justify, and defend their thinking with the other group members. This teaches students the power of defending and justifying their thinking with evidence and proof.	*Why did you do that?* *Is that true?* *Why did you use that strategy?* *Can you prove it?* *Are you sure?* *How do you know?* *Why did you use that model?* *Does that make sense?* *Do you agree or disagree, and why or why not?* *How is your thinking like Tom's?* *Is there another way?*

Figure 4.10 Group Participation

What It Is	What It Does	What It Sounds Like
Students write down or model their thinking and then share it with the whole group.	This allows students to focus on their own strategies and models, jot them down, and then share them. This teaches students the power of justifying and defending their thinking.	*Use a model to show . . .* *Illustrate your strategy.* *On your white boards, show us . . .* *In your guided math journal, show your thinking with numbers, words, or pictures . . . be ready to share it with the group. . . .*

Figure 4.11 Wait Time

What It Is	What It Does	What It Sounds Like
Teachers and students give each other 20–30 seconds of uninterrupted time to think, write, or draw about what they are doing. This is done after the question is asked and then also when the answer is given. Students should be given the time to think about the answer and then respond to it.	This allows students the time to gather their thoughts, to clarify their thinking for themselves, and just to think. It gives students more time to process what is happening. It teaches them the power of stopping to think instead of rushing into a conversation.	*Ok, now I am going to ask some questions, but I want you to take some think time before you answer.* *Terri just gave an answer. Let's think about what she just said before we respond.* *Show me with a silent hand signal when you are ready.* *Let's give everyone some time to think about this. . . .* *Is everybody ready to share or do you need more time . . . ? Show me with a hand signal. . . .*

Figure 4.12 Making Connections

What It Is	What It Does	What It Sounds Like
Teachers and students are asking each other to make connections with what has been said at the table.	It requires students to listen to each other and think about how what they did connects to what someone else did. This teaches students the power of making connections with each other's thinking.	*How is that the same as what Marta did?* *How is that different from what Joe did?* *This is like what Trini did . . .* *How are these models the same and how are they different?* *How are these strategies the same and how are they different?*

Figure 4.13 Partner Talk

What It Is	What It Does	What It Sounds Like
Students talk with their math partners about the math before they share out with the group. They might even draw or write something to share out.	This allows students to think out the math with each other, try to make sense of it, and then be able to explain it to the whole group. This teaches students the power of working together to make sense of the math.	*Turn and talk to your partner.* *Tell your partner what you think and why you think that.* *Show and explain to your partner what you did.* *Defend your thinking to your partner.*

Figure 4.14 Prompting for Student Participation

What It Is	What It Does	What It Sounds Like
The teacher or the students encourage each other to participate in the conversation.	This allows students to participate with each other in the discussion. It openly asks for participation that builds on what has just been said. This teaches students the power of participating in a discussion.	*Who would like to add to that?* *Who wants to say more?* *How did you do it that is the same or different from the way Hong did it?* *Is there another model?* *Is there another strategy?* *Is there another way?*

Figure 4.15 Clarifying One's Own Thinking

What It Is	What It Does	What It Sounds Like
Teachers and students take the time to clarify their thinking.	It allows students to expand on their original thoughts. It requires them to give more examples, show more models, and explain at a deeper level.	*Can you explain that further?* *Can you tell us more?* *What does that mean?* *Can you show us a model and explain it?* *Can you illustrate your strategy and explain it?*

Figure 4.16 Reflecting/Revising/Probing

What It Is	What It Does	What It Sounds Like
The teacher and the students take time to reflect on what has been said and possibly revise their thinking.	This gives students an opportunity to rethink about what they have just done. They get permission to change their minds. It teaches them the power of reflecting on and revising their work.	*Did anybody change their mind?* *Did anybody revise their thinking?* *Now that you see this model, what do you think?* *Now that you see this strategy, what do you think?* *Thinking about what Jamal just said, how does that help us with our thinking?*

It is very important to use different talk moves with students guided math group in order to scaffold the discussions. The previous structures can definitely get you started doing this. It is important to plan for what you want to work on so that it isn't just random conversations. You should be explicit with students when teaching these structures. For example, you might say, "Today we are working on wait time. I want you to think about giving each other the time to think as we talk. Remember, just because you are ready doesn't mean your neighbor is yet."

Key Points

♦ Questions Matter
♦ Plan for Great Questions
♦ DOK Questions
♦ Questions That Pique Curiosity
♦ Student-to-Student Conversations
♦ Scaffolding Questions for ELLs
♦ Five Talk Moves and More

Summary

We must plan for good conversations. Planning matters. We must think about the ways in which we want our students to engage with each other and then actively do that in our groups. Think about the level of rigor of our questions. Think about what kinds of questions pique curiosity and how we get students to engage with each other respectfully, confidently, and competently. We must stay conscious of scaffolding our questions for ELLs so that everyone has a way to enter into the conversations. We need to consider the different types of talk moves that allow us to have rigorous, engaging, and productive conversations.

Reflection Questions

1. What stands out for you in this chapter?
2. What will you enact right away?
3. What questions do you still have?

References

Chapin, S., O'Connor, C., & Anderson, N. (2009). *Classroom discussions: Using math talk to help students learn, grades K–6* (2nd ed.). Sausalito, CA: Math Solutions Publications.

Daro, P. *Against "answer-getting."* Retrieved February 5, 2021 from https://vimeo.com/79916037

Kazemi, E., & Hintz, A. (2014). *Intentional talk: How to structure and lead productive mathematical discussions.* Portland: Steinhouse.

NCTM. (1991). *Professional standards for teaching mathematics.* Reston, VA: NCTM.

O'Connell, S., & O'Connor, K. (2007). *Introduction to communication, grades 3–5.* Heinemann. Retrieved November 24, 2020, from https://mathsolutions.com/math-talk/; http://fspsscience.pbworks.com/w/file/fetch/80214878/Leveled_20Questions_20for_20ELLs; www.aworldoflanguagelearners.com/asking-answering-questions-with-ells/

5

Small-Group Fluency Lessons

Basic fact fluency is a major part of second grade. Students should come into the grade having fluency within 10. However, often times, these facts need to be reviewed and firmed up, and then the emphasis is learning the other strategies, such as doubles, doubles plus 1 and 2, bridging 10, half facts, and higher addition and subtraction facts. Research says that we should devote at least 10 minutes a day to fluency practice (NCEE, 2009). It should be done as energizers and routines, in workstations, and sometimes as guided math lessons. Teachers should integrate fluency work throughout the year because students learn their basic facts at different times.

Fluency is a multidimensional concept. We like to think of it as a four-legged stool: accuracy, flexibility, efficiency, and instant recall. Although we eventually want students to have instant recall, we need them to understand what they are doing with the numbers first. The emphasis in the guided math group is to do a variety of engaging, interactive, rigorous, student-friendly activities that build a fundamental understanding of how numbers are in relationship with each other. The research resoundingly states that computational fluency is multidimensional (speed and accuracy, flexibility, and efficiency) (Brownell & Chazal, 1935; Brownell, 1956, 1956/1987; Kilpatrick, Swafford, & Findell, 2001; National Council of Teachers of Mathematics, 2000).

As you explore the facts with the students, be sure to do concrete, pictorial, and abstract activities with them. There should be several ways for students to practice that are fun and challenging. Students should keep track of how they are doing as well.

Research Note 🔍

- There has been a long debate on traditional fact-based instruction centered on memorization and strategy-based instruction centered on number sense and using strategies. Strategy-based instruction helps students to understand the math they are doing and to do it with eventual flexibility, efficiency, automaticity, and accuracy (Baroody, Purpura, Eiland, Reid, & Paliwal, 2016; Henry & Brown, 2008; Thornton, 1978).
- Boaler (2015) argues that the emphasis of rote memorization through repetition and timed testing is "Unnecessary and damaging."
- Several scholars have promoted engaging practice through strategy-based games and activities that can scaffold learning of basic facts (Van de Walle, 2007; Godfrey & Stone, 2013; Kling & Bay-Williams; Newton, 2016; Newton, Record, & Mello, 2020).

In this chapter we will explore:

- Bridge Ten Addition
- Bridge Ten Subtraction
- Doubles Plus 1
- Half Facts

Overview

Figure 5.1 Overview

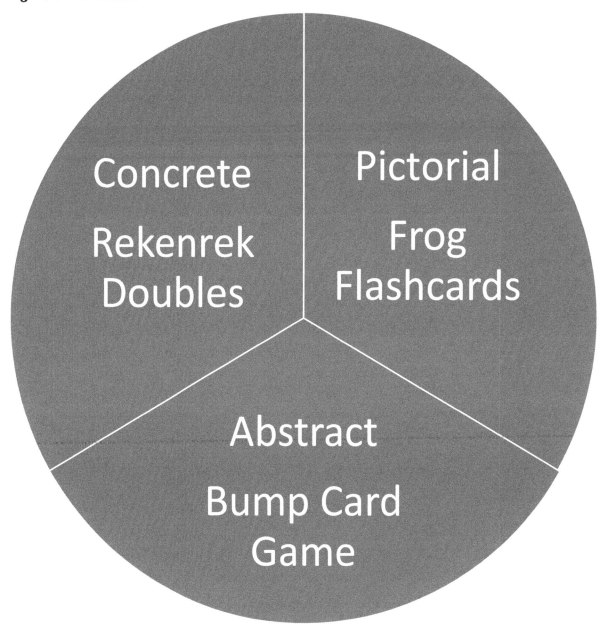

Figure 5.2 Planning Template

Exploring Bridging Ten Facts	
Big Idea: Addition is joining together. **Enduring Understanding:** We can use different strategies to solve addition problems. Bridging through ten is an addition strategy when working with larger numbers. **Essential Question:** How can bridging 10 help us to add larger numbers more efficiently? **Content Question:** What is bridging 10? **I can statement:** I can add using different strategies.	**Materials** ♦ Tools: Rekenrek ♦ Rekenrek Paper ♦ Templates: Ten Frame ♦ Cards ♦ Crayons **Questions** ♦ What does it mean to bridge 10? ♦ Which number do we start with? ♦ What is the sum? ♦ What is an addend?
Cycle of Engagement **Concrete:** Rekenrek **Pictorial:** Number Wand **Abstract:** Play Largest Sum 8 + 6 14	**Vocabulary & Language Frames** Count on Addends Sum Total Strategy Model Start with _____ and count on. The sum of ___ and ____ is _____.

Figure 5.3 Differentiation

Three Differentiated Lessons
In this series of lessons, students are working on the concept of *bridging through ten* with different models. They are developing this concept through concrete activities, pictorial activities, and abstract activities. Here are some things to think about as you do these lessons.

Emerging	On Grade Level	Above Grade Level
Review counting to add. Use number paths and number lines so that students can see that benchmark number 10.	Students should understand how to bridge 7, 8, or 9 to make a 10 and add efficiently.	Expand the number range. Students will work on this concept with adding 2-digit and 1-digit numbers as well as adding 2-digit and 2-digit numbers.

 Looking for Misunderstandings and Common Errors

When students are first learning addition, they will use counting strategies. We want students to develop other strategies such as bridging 10 when they are adding 7, 8, or 9. They need to have plenty of opportunities where they understand the concept of bridging 10 so that they build it into the repertoire of strategies. Remember to play tons of games where students have to use different strategies such as war, bingo, bump, and tic tac toe.

Figure 5.4 Anchor Chart

We can model bridging ten in many ways!
*

Twenty Frame:
Here we have 7 + 9. We can see if we just make the 9 a 10 we have 10 + 6 which is an easier problem.

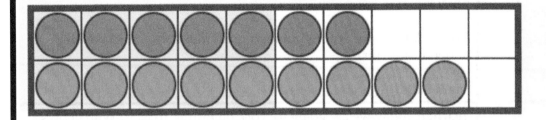

On the Rekenrek we can see 8 + 7 can be made easier. We can make the 8 a 10. Then we have 10 + 5. We could also think 8 + 8 is 16, so 8 + 7 is 15.

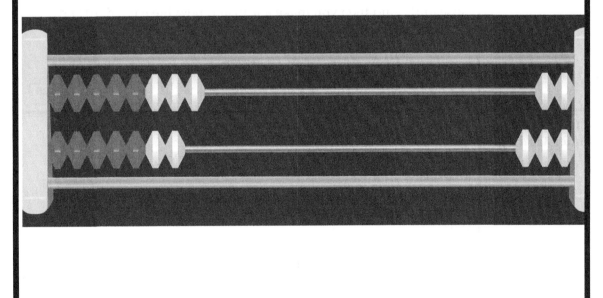

Concrete Lesson

Figure 5.5 Concrete Introduction

	Introduction
Launch	**Teacher:** Today we are going to work on bridging 10 with different models. **Vocabulary:** count on, big number, small number, strategy, model, addend, sum, total **Math Talk:** _____ and _____ make _____. _____ + _____ = _____
Model	**Teacher:** Today we are going to work on bridge 10 facts. Who knows what it means to bridge 10? **Jamal:** It means to use 10 to make the problem easier. **Teacher:** Yes. Why? **Tami:** Because like say you had 6 + 9 . . . you start with 9 because it is close to 10. And then you make it a 10 and now the 6 is a 5. 10 and 5 is 15! Easy-peasy. | 1 | 2 | 3 | 4 | 5 | 6 | 7 | 8 | 9 | 10 | 11 | 12 | 13 | 14 | 15 | 16 | 17 | 18 | 19 | 20 |
Checking for Understanding	**Teacher:** Excellent example. Who has another one? **Kelli:** Like if I had 9 + 5 then I could go 10 + 4. You give one and you take one. **Teacher:** Ok, who has an example of where the hop-on frog would start? **Mark:** Like if he always looks for 7, 8, or 9 to make a 10.

Figure 5.6 Student Activity

	Student Activity
Guided Practice/Checking for Understanding	**Teacher:** Ok, smarty pants . . . I am going to hand out the frog and the number line. You will each get one. Take your cards and solve the problems. I am going to watch you and ask questions. Be ready to share your thinking with the group. **Todd:** I had 7 + 6. I know that is 13 because 6 + 6 is 12 and 1 more is 13. **Teacher:** High five! Excellent strategy. **Mary:** I could hop to 10 and then hop 3 more. **Teacher:** Great thinking! **7 + 6** | 1 | 2 | 3 | 4 | 5 | 6 | 7 | 8 | 9 | 10 | 11 | 12 | 13 | 14 | 15 | 16 | 17 | 18 | 19 | 20 | **Melissa:** I had 9 + 4. I started on 9 to get to 10. That was 1 hop. I have 3 more hops. I am at 13.
Set Up for Independent Practice	*Everyone starts practicing. The teacher asks the students questions individually. Then, the teacher goes around the circle and has each student share one of their problems and explain what they did. At the end, the teacher asks students to talk about the math, and if it is easy or tricky.*

Figure 5.7 Lesson Close

Close
♦ What did we do today? ♦ What was the math we were practicing? ♦ What were we doing with the count on strategy? ♦ Was this easy or tricky? ♦ Turn to a partner and state one thing you learned today.

Figure 5.8 Cards

Pull a flashcard and hop to 10. Then hop the rest of the way. There are many strategies, we are just practicing this one today.

4 + 7	9 + 2
5 + 7	8 + 3
9 + 7	5 + 8
9 + 2	4 + 9
1 + 9	4 + 8
3 + 9	8 + 7

Pictorial Lesson

Figure 5.9 Pictorial Introduction

Introduction	
Launch	**Teacher:** Today we are going to work on bridging 10 with different models. **Vocabulary:** count on, big number, small number, strategy, model, addend, sum, total **Math Talk:** _____ and _____ make _____. _____ + _____ = _____
Model	**Teacher:** Today we are going to continue to work on bridging 10 facts. I am going to give you a set of cards to work with a partner. You are going to show your partner how you would solve the problem. I am going to listen in to your conversations and ask questions. Later on, we are going to share out to the whole group. What can you tell me about these flashcards? $$2 + 9^* =$$ 0 1 2 3 4 5 6 7 8 9 10 11 12 13 14 15 16 17 18 19 20 Get to 10. Hop on.
Checking for Understanding	**Tim:** They have a number line. That star thing means get to a 10. **Melissa:** So 9 plus 1 is 10 and then 1 more is 11. **Teacher:** Yes, you can use the number line to help you break apart the numbers.

Figure 5.10 Student Activity

	Student Activity
Guided Practice/ Checking for Understanding	Students work in pairs or triads and explain their thinking to each other. $$4 + 8^* =$$ 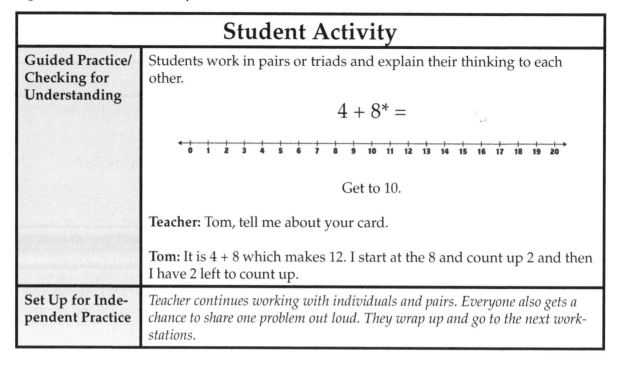 Get to 10. **Teacher:** Tom, tell me about your card. **Tom:** It is 4 + 8 which makes 12. I start at the 8 and count up 2 and then I have 2 left to count up.
Set Up for Independent Practice	*Teacher continues working with individuals and pairs. Everyone also gets a chance to share one problem out loud. They wrap up and go to the next workstations.*

Figure 5.11 Lesson Close

Close
♦ What did we do today? ♦ What was the math we were practicing? ♦ What were we doing with our flashcards? ♦ Was this easy or tricky? ♦ Turn to a partner and state one thing you learned today.

Abstract Lesson

Figure 5.12 Abstract Introduction

	Introduction
Launch	**Teacher:** Today we are going to work on bridging 10 with different models. **Vocabulary:** count on, big number, small number, strategy, model, addend, sum, total **Math Talk:** _____ and _____ make _____. _____ + _____ = _____
Model	**Teacher:** Today we are going to continue to work on bridge 10 facts. Today's game is "Biggest Sum." You are going to play with a partner or in a triad. Each person picks a card, calculates the total, and then compares the sum. Whoever has the largest sum wins the cards. Whoever has the most cards when all the cards are done wins the game.
Checking for Understanding	**Teacher:** Who can tell me how to play the game? **Todd:** You get a partner and you each pull a card. Whoever has the biggest sum wins the cards. **Mary:** When all the cards are gone, whoever has the most cards wins!

Figure 5.13 Lesson Close

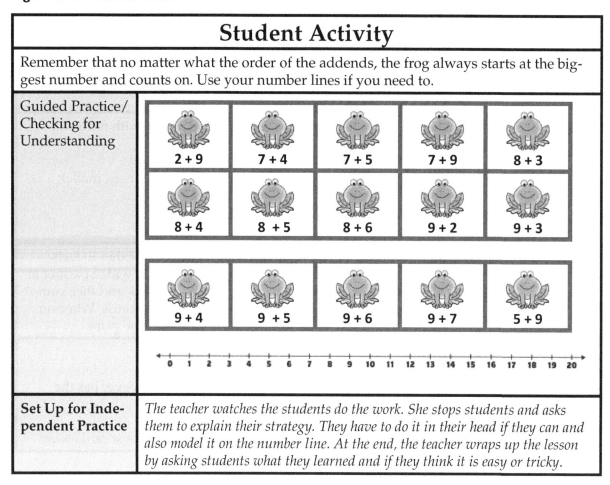

	Student Activity
	Remember that no matter what the order of the addends, the frog always starts at the biggest number and counts on. Use your number lines if you need to.
Guided Practice/ Checking for Understanding	2 + 9 7 + 4 7 + 5 7 + 9 8 + 3 8 + 4 8 + 5 8 + 6 9 + 2 9 + 3 9 + 4 9 + 5 9 + 6 9 + 7 5 + 9 0 1 2 3 4 5 6 7 8 9 10 11 12 13 14 15 16 17 18 19 20
Set Up for Independent Practice	*The teacher watches the students do the work. She stops students and asks them to explain their strategy. They have to do it in their head if they can and also model it on the number line. At the end, the teacher wraps up the lesson by asking students what they learned and if they think it is easy or tricky.*

Close
♦ What did we do today? ♦ What was the math we were practicing? ♦ Was this easy or tricky? ♦ Turn to a partner and state one thing you learned today.

Section Summary

In this section, we have looked at concrete, pictorial, and abstract activities that help scaffold students' understanding of bridging through ten addition strategies. Students should also practice these strategies using ten frames, rekenreks, and number lines. Students should also practice by walking out the problems on number lines and using interactive number lines where they can start at the large number and move the bead on it. They should play several board games, card games, and dice games where they work on the strategy.

Bridge Ten Subtraction

Overview

Figure 5.14 Overview

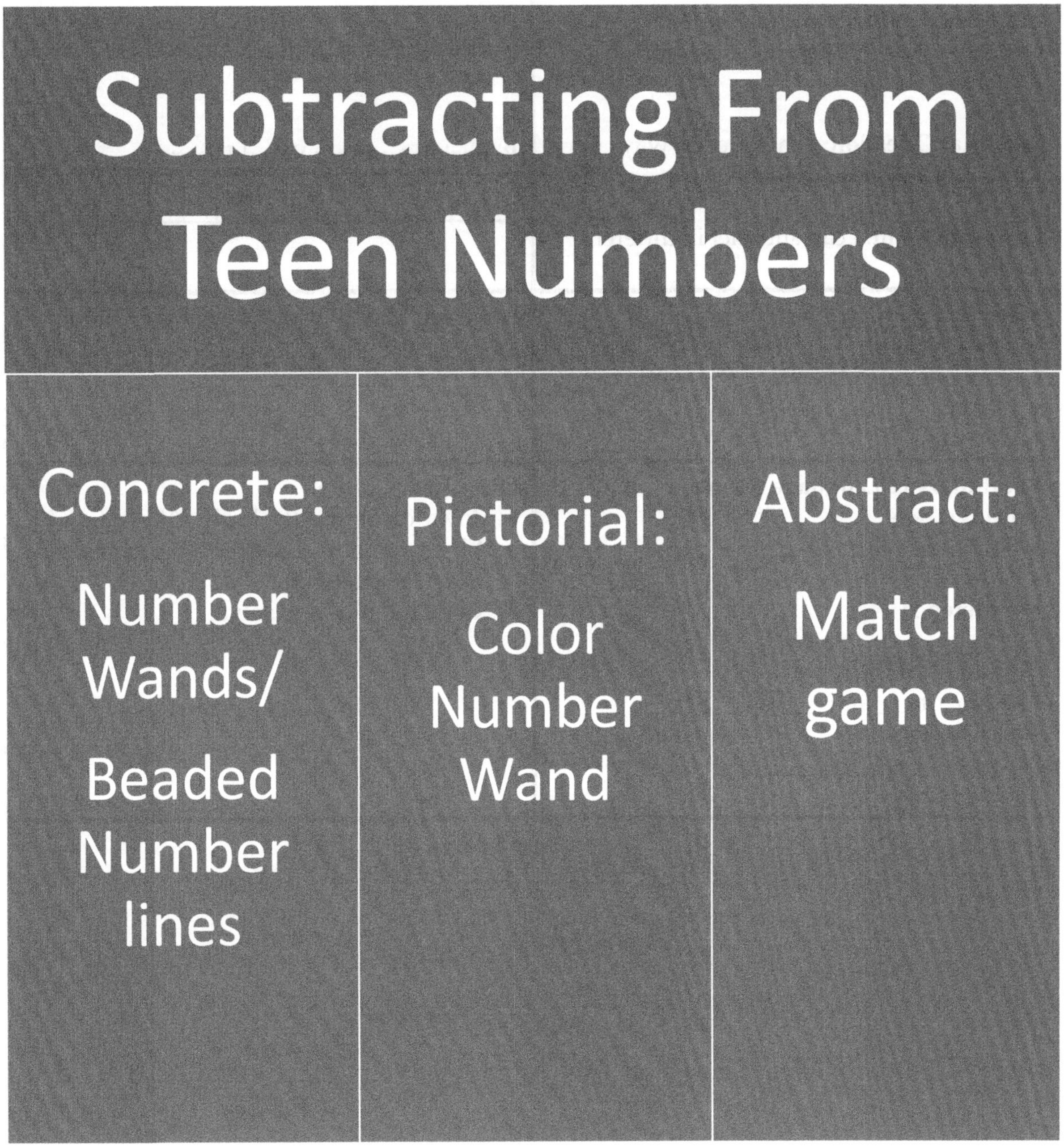

Subtracting From Teen Numbers
Concrete:
Number Wands/ Beaded Number lines
Pictorial:
Color Number Wand
Abstract:
Match game

Figure 5.15 Planning Template

Subtracting From the Teens

Big Idea: There are many different strategies for subtracting.

Enduring Understanding: Students will understand and be able to use different strategies.

Essential Question: What are the ways to subtract from teen numbers?

I can statement: I can subtract in different ways.

Cycle of Engagement

Concrete: Number Wand

Pictorial: Number Wand Diagram

Materials
+ Tools: Cubes
+ Templates: Ten Frame
+ Cards
+ Crayons

Abstract: Match Addends and the Difference

7

12 – 5

Vocabulary & Language Frames
+ Bridge Tens
+ Addends
+ Sum
+ Difference

___ and ___ make _____.
The sum of ___ and ____ is _____.
The difference of ___ and ___ make _____.
My strategy is _____.
My model was _____.

Questions
+ How do you use the bridge 10 strategy?
+ What are some strategies for subtracting from teen numbers?
+ Name two ways to solve _____

Figure 5.16 Differentiation

Three Differentiated Lessons		
In this series of lessons, students are working on the concept of *subtracting from teen numbers* using a variety of strategies. They are developing this concept through concrete activities, pictorial activities, and abstract activities. Here are some things to think about as you do these lessons.		
Emerging Level	**On Grade Level**	**Above Grade Level**
Review subtracting within and from 10. Use different manipulatives to show how to make 10, including the rekenrek, the ten frame, and Cuisenaire™ rods.	Students should work with the twenty frame. They should play many games and do missing addend problems.	Expand the number range.

 Looking for Misunderstandings and Common Errors

Make ten facts are foundational. Having a variety of strategies for subtracting using ten as a bridge number is a strategy that is commonly taught and used throughout the world. Spend as much time as students need to make sure that everyone learns how to do this. They should do a great deal of work with looking at the combinations and then a great deal of work to see it visually with the ten frame.

Concrete Lesson

Figure 5.17 Concrete Introduction

	Introduction
Launch	**Teacher:** Today we are going to work on using ten to subtract from bigger numbers. Our goal is to learn different ways how to "bridge 10." **Vocabulary:** combinations, ten, ten friends, decompose, compose We have an anchor chart here to help us think about ten friends. The one we made in whole group. **Vocabulary:** count on, big number, small number, strategy, model, addend, sum, total **Math Talk:** _____ and ____ make _____. _____ + _____ = _____ *The teacher passes out number lines to every child.* **Teacher:** Let's look at them. What do you notice? 14 − 8 Look at my problem. Look at all your tools. Who could tell me a way to take 8 away from 14? | 1 | 2 | 3 | 4 | 5 | 6 | 7 | 8 | 9 | 10 | 11 | 12 | 13 | 14 | 15 | 16 | 17 | 18 | 19 | 20 | **Mike:** I could count back. I'll model it with the frog. **Teacher:** Show me how. *Mike counts back by ones.* **Claire:** You could also count up. Like hold 8 in your head and then count to 14. I would get 6. I will model it with the frog.

Model	**Teacher:** Yes. You could do that too. Those are some good ways. We have been looking at those ways during our energizers. I want to talk about another way today. Like if I think about 10 it can help me. Watch. If I get to 10 and then *hop on* it might make it easier. For example, you all know your ten friends, so 8 and what make 10?
	Students: 2.
	Teacher: And then how many more to hop on to 14?
	Mike: 4.
Checking for Understanding	**Teacher:** Let's try another one: 15 – 7.
	Hope: 8 + 2 is 10 and then 5 more is 15. So 2 and 5 is 7.
	Teacher: Yes. See, 10 can help us do it more quickly if we know how to get to 10. We could also do it by counting back. Who could tell me how that might look?
	Marta: 15 – 5 gets us to 10 and then 2 more to 8. 5 and 2 make 7.
	Tom: I like to count up. It's easier.
	Chrissy: Me too.

Figure 5.18 Student Activity

Student Activity	
Guided Practice/ Checking for Understanding	**Teacher:** Ok, I am going to give each one of you a problem. You can use any method or tool you want, I just want you to explain your strategy and model it for us. **Luke:** I got 16 – 9. I counted up. 1 more is 10 and then 6 more is 16. So it is 7. I did that on the number line. 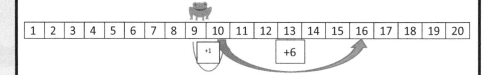 **Marta:** I got 17 – 8. I did 2 more is 10 and 7 more is 17 so that is 9. **Teacher:** I want to show you folks another way to think about it as well. You could add 2 to both numbers to make an easier problem. What would happen if I added 2 to both numbers? **Chris:** It would be 19 – 10 and that makes 9. And it is the same answer. **Teacher:** Why? *Nobody answers.* **Teacher:** I want you guys to try that strategy sometimes. What happens if when you are subtracting you change the problem into an easier one? Will you get the same answer? **Don:** Let's try another one to see. **Teacher:** Ok, 14 – 8. **Don:** Ok, if we add 2 to make it 16 – 10 we get 6. **Marta:** And 8 plus 2 is 10 plus 4 more is 14. . . so we added 6. **Don:** It's the same! **Teacher:** Yep . . . who can tell me why? I want you to play with it and we will talk about it more the next time I meet you folks.

	Kelly: I got 12 − 5. I was thinking 12 − 6 is 6 so 12 take away 5 has to be 7?
		1	2	3	4	5	6	7	8	9	10	11	12	13	14	15	16	17	18	19	20	
	Teacher: Tell me more about that.
	Kelly: Well, you are taking away 1 less so it has to be 7.
	Teacher: How could you check your thinking?
	Kelly: I could count back 12, 11, 10, 9, 8, 7 . . . yes, I'm right.
	Teacher: Ok, what were we doing today?
	Tammy: Subtracting from the teen numbers. It's kinda tricky.
Set Up for Independent Practice	**Teacher:** What is tricky?
	Kelly: Like the counting back is harder than counting up. You get the same answer. It's easier to add up.
	Teacher: Can you really add when you are subtracting?
	Missy: Yes. We just did it.

Figure 5.19 Lesson Close

Close
♦ What did we do today?   ♦ What was the math we were practicing?   ♦ Was this easy or tricky?   ♦ Turn to a partner and state one thing you learned today.

Figure 5.20 Cards

14 – 8	12 – 7
13 – 5	12 – 9
11 – 8	11 – 4
14 – 9	11 – 3
11 – 9	11 – 2
12 – 3	11 – 5
12 – 4	11 – 6
17 – 8	12 – 8
13 – 4	17 – 9
13 – 5	13 – 8
15 – 7	16 – 9
14 – 5	14 – 6
15 – 6	16 – 7

Pictorial Lesson

Figure 5.21 Pictorial Introduction

	Introduction
Launch	**Teacher:** Today we are going to work on using ten to subtract from bigger numbers. Our goal is to learn different ways how to "bridge 10." **Vocabulary:** count on, big number, small number, strategy, model, addend, sum, total **Math Talk:** _____ and ____ make _____. _____ + _____ = _____
Model	**Teacher:** Today we are going to continue to work on subtracting from teen numbers. (*The teacher passes out number wands to every child.*) What do you remember about them? *Students should talk about what they did last time.* **Teacher:** Today we are going to break apart our wands and then record our work. Step 1: Watch what I do. Here is my number wand. I am going to use it to look at how I can use ten to help me subtract big numbers. Step 2: My problem is 15 – 7 So, I can say I am going to take away 5 so that I can get to a 10. Then from 10 I need to break off 2 more.
Checking for Understanding	Step 3: So I have 8 left. Now I am going to record my work on the cube template. **Teacher:** Let's do one together.

Figure 5.22 Student Activity

Student Activity	
Guided Practice/ Checking for Understanding	*Students go around and break their ten wand, record their work, and explain it to the group.* **Lilly:** My problem is 15 – 9 I took away 5. Now I have 10 left. I am going to take away 4 more. So I have 6 left from my 15 stick. Step 3: Now I am going to record my work on the cube template.
Set Up for Independent Practice	*After everyone has had an opportunity to share, the teacher wraps up the lesson. Students share out their thinking and then go into station work.*

Figure 5.23 Lesson Close

Close
◆ What did we do today? ◆ What was the math we were practicing? ◆ What were we doing with our number wands? ◆ Was this easy or tricky? ◆ Turn to a partner and state one thing you learned today.

Figure 5.24 Recording Sheet

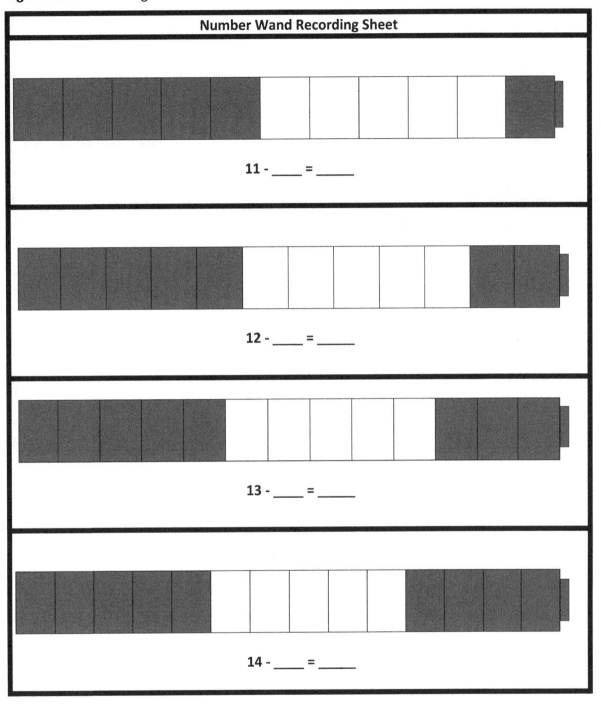

Number Wand Recording Sheet

11 - _____ = _____

12 - _____ = _____

13 - _____ = _____

14 - _____ = _____

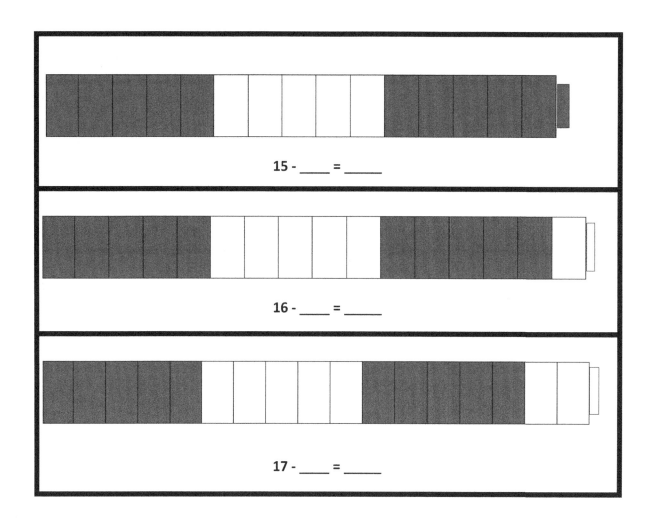

15 - _____ = _____

16 - _____ = _____

17 - _____ = _____

Abstract Lesson

Figure 5.25 Abstract Introduction

	Introduction
Launch	**Teacher:** Today we are going to work on using ten to subtract from bigger numbers. Our goal is to learn different ways how to "bridge 10." **Vocabulary:** count on, big number, small number, strategy, model, addend, sum, total **Math Talk:** _____ and _____ make _____. _____ + _____ = _____
Model	**Teacher:** Today we are going to continue to work bridging 10. We are going to play a card game today. Who can remind us what it means to "bridge 10?" **Tami:** Like 11 – 9, we could count up to 10 and add 1 more. **Teacher:** Who can tell me another way to "bridge 10?" **Student:** Like 15 – 9. We could take away 10 and add 1 back too. **Teacher:** Yes, that is another good strategy. Ok, today we are going to see how well you all know how to bridge 10 or use other strategies. Today we are going to play a card game. It is a match game. We have 20 cards and they are all turned face down. We will take turns trying to find all the matching subtraction problems and their difference. If you get stuck, you can look at our anchor chart. To start, we are going to each roll the dice. Whoever has the largest number starts the game. Then we take turns. The person on your left goes after you and we continue going in that direction.
Checking for Understanding	**Teacher:** Who can explain the game? **Marta:** It's a card game. We are looking for pairs of the expression and the difference. It's like concentration. When you get a match, you win that pair. **Jamal:** Whoever gets the most matches wins at the end.

Figure 5.26 Student Activity

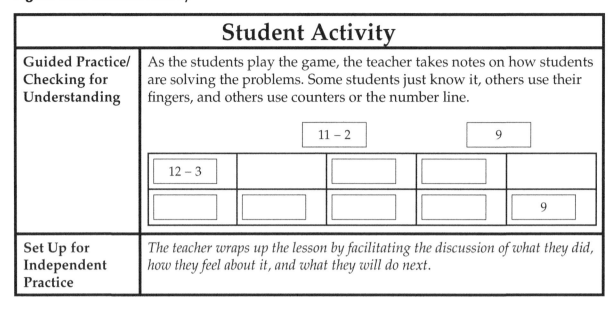

Student Activity	
Guided Practice/ Checking for Understanding	As the students play the game, the teacher takes notes on how students are solving the problems. Some students just know it, others use their fingers, and others use counters or the number line.
Set Up for Independent Practice	*The teacher wraps up the lesson by facilitating the discussion of what they did, how they feel about it, and what they will do next.*

Figure 5.27 Lesson Close

Close

♦ What did we do today?
♦ What was the math we were practicing?
♦ Was this easy or tricky?
♦ Turn to a partner and state one thing you learned today.

Figure 5.28 Cards

1	2	3	4	5
6	7	8	9	10
1	2	3	4	5
6	7	8	9	10

15 – 6	16 – 9	17 – 9
15 – 8	16 – 7	17 – 8
14 – 9	13 – 5	12 – 4
14 – 8	11 – 3	12 – 8
13 – 6	12 – 5	11 – 2

Section Summary

Bridging ten to subtract is an important strategy that students should get comfortable with in second grade. There are lots of prerequisite skills. Students have to know how to count back or up. They have to know how to decompose numbers. They should know their combinations of ten. The strategy is difficult if they are lacking some of these prerequisite skills. Too often, textbooks rush this skill and some students aren't yet ready for it. Know your students. When they are ready, start playing around with this strategy.

They will use this throughout the rest of their learning about adding and subtracting multi-digit numbers. There should be many opportunities for students to practice this strategy on the rekenrek, the ten frame, the number wands, and other manipulatives. After students do a great deal of work on the ten frames, they should work with a variety of games where they have to recall the facts.

Doubles Plus 1

Overview

Figure 5.29 Overview

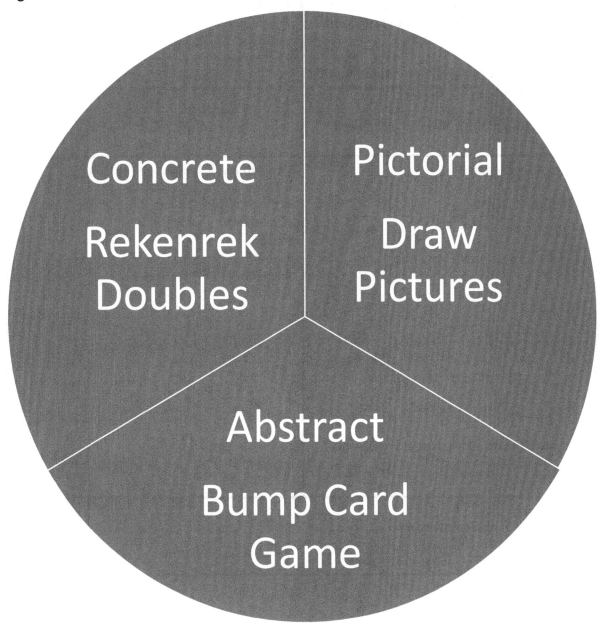

Figure 5.30 Planning Template

Addition Doubles Plus 1	
Big Idea: Addition is joining together. **Enduring Understanding:** We can use different strategies to solve addition problems. Doubles is an addition strategy. **Essential Question:** What are different addition strategies? **I can statement:** I can add using different strategies.	**Materials** ♦ Tools: Rekenrek ♦ Rekenrek Paper ♦ Templates: Ten Frame ♦ Cards ♦ Crayons
Cycle of Engagement **Concrete:** Rekenrek **Pictorial:** _____ + _____ **Abstract:: Match Addends and the Sum** | 3 + 4		5 + 6		**Vocabulary & Language Frames** ♦ Doubles ♦ Doubles Plus 1 Facts ♦ Addends ♦ Sum ♦ Total ♦ Strategy ♦ Model ___ and ___ make _____. The sum of ___ and ____ is _____.
Questions ♦ What are doubles plus 1 facts? ♦ Why would we use them? ♦ Can you model a doubles plus 1 fact?	

Figure 5.31 Differentiation

Three Differentiated Lessons		
In this series of lessons, students are working on the concept of doubles plus one facts with different models. They are developing this concept through concrete activities, pictorial activities, and abstract activities. Here are some things to think about as you do these lessons.		
Emerging	**On Grade Level**	**Above Grade Level**
Review adding doubles. Practice making them with tools including the rekenrek, the ten frame, and Cuisenaire™ rods.	In second grade, students should learn to recognize and solve doubles plus 1 facts. Students should work with the ten frame. They should play many games and do missing addend problems.	Expand the number range.

 Looking for Misunderstandings and Common Errors

When you teach doubles plus 1, be sure to have students explore these type of facts on the twenty frame. They can see it quite clearly on that model.

Figure 5.32 Anchor Chart

We can model doubles plus 1 facts in many ways!

Ten Frame:

7 + 8

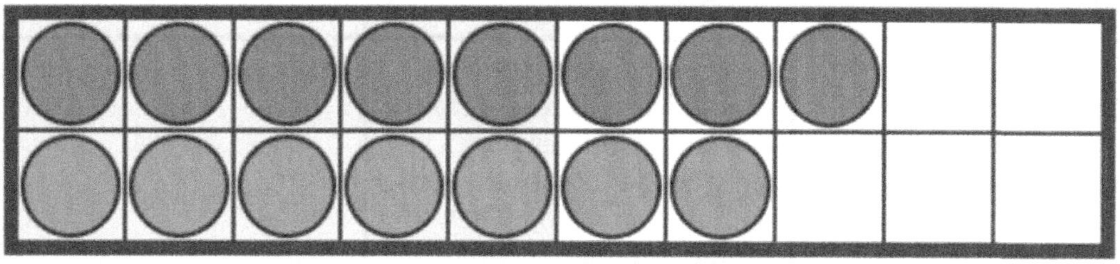

Cuisenaire™ Rod

5 + 6 = 9

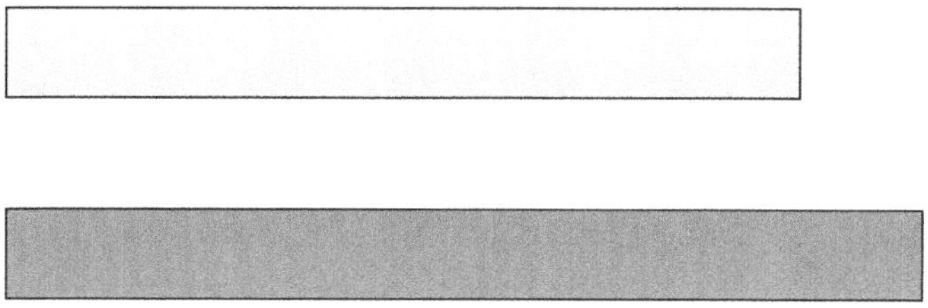

Sketch

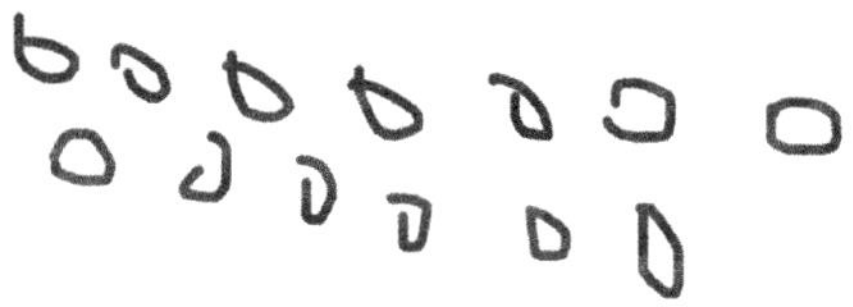

Concrete Lesson

Figure 5.33 Concrete Introduction

Introduction	
Launch	**Teacher:** Today we are going to continue work on adding doubles plus one facts with different models. We will use our virtual models. Let's look at them. What do you notice? **Vocabulary:** doubles, strategy, model, addend, sum, total, doubles plus one **Math Talk:** _____ and ____ make _____. _____ + _____ = _____
Model	**Teacher:** Today we are going to continue exploring doubles plus 1 facts. Who knows what doubles plus 1 facts are? **Jamal:** They are when you add doubles and then there is 1 more. **Teacher:** Yes. Give me an example. **Jamal:** Like 5 + 6. **Teacher:** Does anyone else know any doubles plus 1 facts? **Kelli:** Yes. 2 + 3. **Mark:** 3 + 4. **Teacher:** How are all these facts alike? Let's look at them. (*Teacher writes down the facts on the white board.*) **Mark:** They are like the same number but then there is 1 more. **Missy:** You could also show it on the rekenrek.

Checking for Understanding	**Teacher:** Everybody pick a model and show me a doubles plus 1 fact? **Raul:** I did one on the twenty frame. 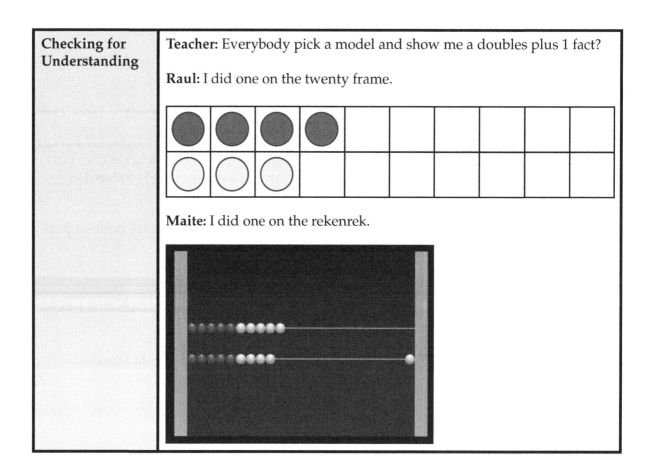 **Maite:** I did one on the rekenrek.

Figure 5.34 Student Activity

	# Student Activity
Guided Practice/ Checking for Understanding	The teacher passes out addition doubles plus 1 facts. Students pull a card and act out their problems however they want. The students each get a chance to share their problem and explain how they solved it. **Maria:** I had 8 + 9. That makes 17 because 8 + 8 is 16 and 1 more is 17. I just knew it. **Todd:** I had 4 + 5. That makes 9. *Everyone goes around and shares their thinking. This is a group that is ready for this concept at this point in the year and so the teacher introduces the rekenrek paper in the same lesson.* **Teacher:** Who thinks they could solve their doubles fact and then draw it on the rekenrek paper? *All the children raise their hand.* **Tina:** I know how. See, if I pull 8 + 7 I model it. Then I draw that. Just like we do on the rug. 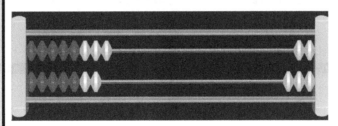 **Teacher:** Yes, let's do that. (teacher passes out the rekenrek paper). Name: Date: Draw What You Did on the Rekenrek! 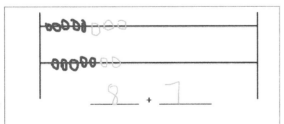
Set Up for Independent Practice	*Everyone models their problem and shares their thinking with a neighbor. Then, the teacher wraps up the lesson by facilitating the discussion of what they did, how they feel about it, and what they will do next.*

Figure 5.35 Lesson Close

Close
◆ What did we do today? ◆ What was the math we were practicing? ◆ Was this easy or tricky? ◆ Turn to a partner and state one thing you learned today.

Figure 5.36 Cards

0 + 1	5 + 6
1 + 2	2 + 3
3 + 4	4 + 5
1 + 0	6 + 5
2 + 1	3 + 2
4 + 3	5 + 4

Pictorial Lesson

Figure 5.37 Pictorial Introduction

	Introduction
Launch	**Teacher:** Today we are going to continue work on adding doubles plus 1 facts with different models. We will use our virtual models. Let's look at them. What do you notice? **Vocabulary:** doubles, strategy, model, addend, sum, total **Math Talk:** _____ and ____ make _____. _____ + _____ = _____
Model	**Teacher:** Today we are going to continue to work on doubles plus 1 facts. We are going to play a concentration game. You all know how to play concentration. You and your partner will get a deck of cards. You will turn them face down and then take turns trying to find the matches. We are matching doubles plus 1 models and their equations. ┌─────────┐ ┌─────────┐ ┌─────────┐ ┌─────────┐ │ 4 + 3 │ │ ▓▓▓ │ │ │ │ │ └─────────┘ └─────────┘ └─────────┘ └─────────┘
Checking for Understanding	**Teacher:** Who can explain what we are doing today? **Hong:** We are matching doubles plus 1 facts, the picture and the expression. **Marissa:** What is an expression? **Ted:** It's the numbers like 5 plus 4. **Teacher:** Who has another question? **Grace:** What is a doubles plus 1 fact? **Hong:** Like a double plus 1 more . . . for example 3 plus 3 + 1 or 3 + 4. **Todd:** Ms. Chi said they are neighbor numbers. **Teacher:** What does that mean? **Marissa:** They sit next door to each other on the number line. **Teacher:** Ok, great conversation. Any more questions? If not, let's start!

Figure 5.38 Student Activity

Student Activity

Guided Practice/ Checking for Understanding	Students work in pairs or triads and play doubles plus 1 concentration. As they play, the teacher asks questions and takes notes.
	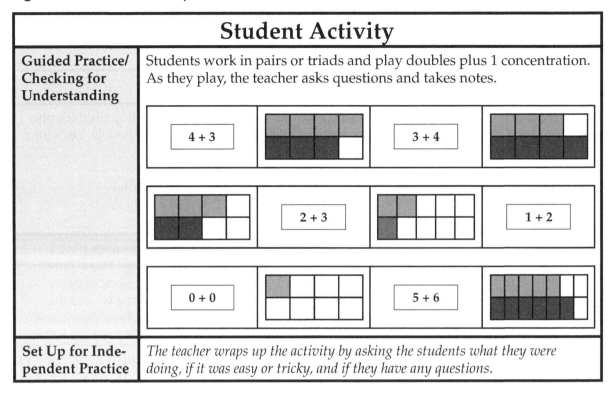
Set Up for Independent Practice	*The teacher wraps up the activity by asking the students what they were doing, if it was easy or tricky, and if they have any questions.*

Figure 5.39 Lesson Close

Close

♦ What did we do today?
♦ What was the math we were practicing?
♦ What were we doing with our number wands?
♦ Was this easy or tricky?
♦ Turn to a partner and state one thing you learned today.

Figure 5.40 Cards

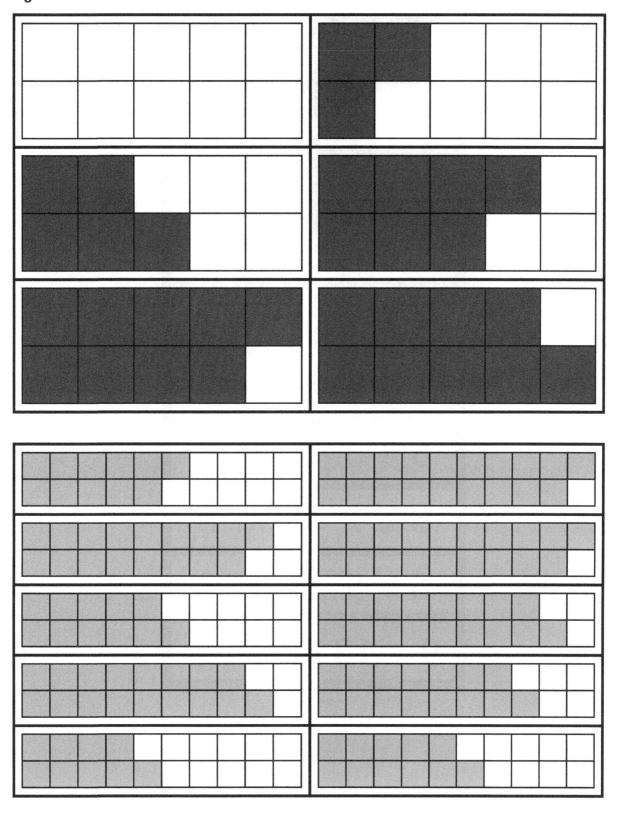

Figure 5.41 Doubles Plus 1 Cards

$0 + 1$	$1 + 0$
$2 + 1$	$3 + 2$
$3 + 4$	$4 + 3$
$1 + 2$	$2 + 3$
$4 + 5$	$5 + 4$
$7 + 6$	$6 + 7$
$6 + 5$	$5 + 6$
$8 + 7$	$7 + 8$
$8 + 9$	$9 + 8$
$9 + 10$	$10 + 9$

Abstract Lesson

Figure 5.42 Abstract Introduction

	Introduction
Launch	**Teacher:** Today we are going to continue work on adding doubles with different models. We will use our virtual models. Let's look at them. What do you notice? **Vocabulary:** doubles, strategy, model, addend, sum, total **Math Talk:** _____ and ____ make _____. _____ + _____ = _____
Model	**Teacher:** Today we are going to continue to work on doubles plus 1 facts. We will be playing a board game today. How many of you like board games? In this game, you will get a doubles plus sum and then you cover up the expression that matches. You add it up and cover the sum. Whoever gets four in a row, wins. **Connect Four** Addition Doubles+1 (1-19) (6+7) (2+3) (8+9) (4+5) (0+1) (4+5) (1+2) (6+7) (2+3) (8+9) (8+9) (6+7) (4+5) (3+4) (2+3) (2+3) (4+5) (0+1) (8+9) (6+7) (1+2) (8+7) (9+10) (6+7) (4+5)
Checking for Understanding	**Teacher:** Who can explain what we are doing today? **Shakhira:** We are playing four in a row. We have to match the expression and the sum. **Kelly:** That's easy we always play four in a row games. **Ted:** Does everybody know what to do? **Teacher:** Ok, any questions? If not, let's start!

Figure 5.43 Student Activity

Student Activity	
Pull a card and double the number add 1 more. Cover the expression that matches the sum. Whoever covers four in a row first wins.	
Guided Practice/ Checking for Understanding	Students work in pairs or triads and play doubles plus 1 concentration. As they play, the teacher asks questions and takes notes. $\boxed{5}$ $\boxed{17}$ Connect Four Addition Doubles+1 (1-19) (6+7) (2+3) (8+9) (4+5) (0+1) (4+5) (1+2) (6+7) (2+3) (8+9) (8+9) (6+7) (4+5) (3+4) (2+3) (2+3) (4+5) (0+1) (8+9) (6+7) (1+2) (8+7) (9+10) (6+7) (4+5) **Teacher:** Tim, explain your thinking. **Tim:** I know that 8 + 8 is 16 so 8 +9 is 17.
Set Up for Independent Practice	**Teacher:** What have we been doing today? **Kiyana:** We have been practicing doubles plus 1 facts. **Nick:** I think this game was tricky. The concentration game was easier because you could see the pictures. **Raj:** Me too. It was tricky. **Teacher:** Who has a strategy that worked for them? **Trish:** I just doubled the number and added 1 more. For example if I got 11. I know 5 + 5 is 10 so 5 plus 6 is 11. **Teacher:** Ok, we will keep working on this. You guys can go to your workstations now.

Figure 5.44 Lesson Close

Close
♦ What did we do today?
♦ What was the math we were practicing?
♦ Was this easy or tricky?
♦ Turn to a partner and state one thing you learned today.

Figure 5.45 Doubles Plus 1 Cards (These can be used for the Connect 4 game instead of dice)

1	3
4	5
7	9
11	13
15	17
19	Free choice

Section Summary

Doubles plus 1 is important. Be sure to scaffold doubles plus 1 by using lots of different visuals such as the rekenrek and the twenty frame. Give students various opportunities to build it, draw it, and then write the equation. For example, they might pull a card, build the fact on a twenty frame, shade it in on a template, and then write the equation. Students should also play individual, partner, and group games, like tic tac toe, bump, and bingo.

Overview

Figure 5.46 Overview

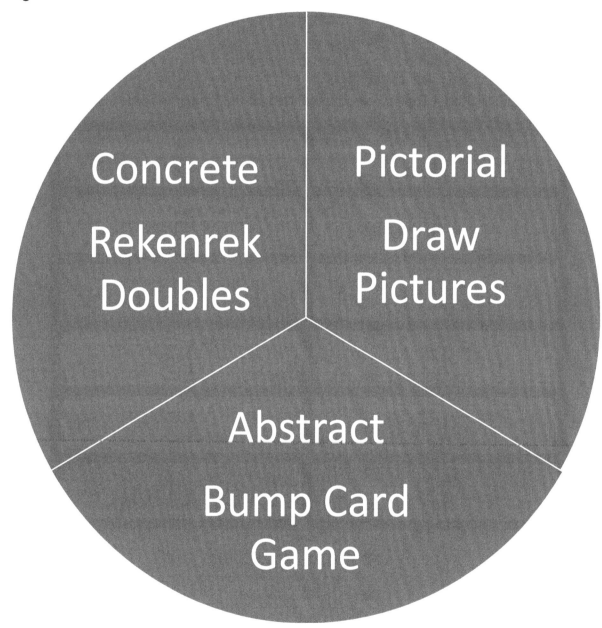

Figure 5.47 Planning Template

Half Facts

Big Idea: Subtraction is about taking away a number from another number. **Enduring Understanding:** There are many different types of subtraction strategies. **Essential Question:** What are different strategies and models to show subtraction? **I can statement:** I can model subtraction in many ways. I can solve subtraction using different strategies.	**Materials** ♦ Tools: Cubes ♦ Templates: Ten Frame ♦ Cards ♦ Crayons
Cycle of Engagement **Concrete:** Subtraction Machine **Pictorial:** Drawing **Abstract:** Match the Difference and the Expression | 4		8 − 4		**Vocabulary & Language Frames** ♦ Doubles ♦ Half Facts ♦ Addends ♦ Sum ♦ Difference ___ and ___ make _____. The sum of ___ and ____ is _____. The difference of ___ is ____ + ____ and ____.
Questions ♦ What is subtraction? What are half facts? ♦ How can you model subtraction? ♦ What does it mean to take away a number? ♦ What is the minus sign?	

Figure 5.48 Differentiation

Three Differentiated Lessons

In this series of lessons, students are working on the concept of modeling half facts with different models. They are developing this concept through concrete activities, pictorial activities, and abstract activities. Here are some things to think about as you do these lessons.

Emerging	On Grade Level	Above Grade Level
There are a substantial number of second graders who come into the grade not having a firm handle on subtraction. In the beginning, make sure that students can subtract within 10. Make sure they know their lower doubles and then all there doubles.	As you are teaching the doubles, teach the half facts. This way students understand the inverse operations. Use different manipulatives to show how to subtract, including the rekenrek, the ten frame, and Cuisenaire™ rods.	Expand the number range.

Looking for Misunderstandings and Common Errors

Spend time on subtraction. In schools, we tend to spend more time on addition than on subtraction. We need to make sure that there is an equal amount of time spent on both operations. By the end of second grade, students are supposed to be fluent with all their basic facts within 20.

Figure 5.49 Anchor Chart

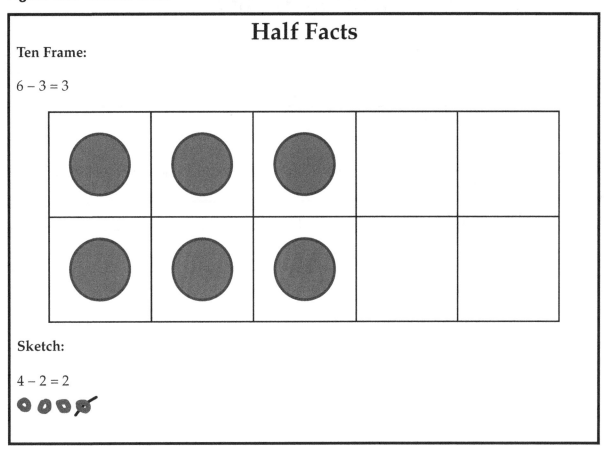

Half Facts

Ten Frame:

6 − 3 = 3

Sketch:

4 − 2 = 2

Concrete Lesson

Figure 5.50 Concrete Introduction

	Introduction
Launch	**Teacher:** Today we are going to work on subtracting with different models. Let's look at them. What do you notice? **Vocabulary:** subtract, take away, minus, difference, big number, small number **Math Talk:** I had _____. I took away _____. I have _____ left.
Model	**Teacher:** Here we have a subtraction machine. Here we have 8 counters in the big box. We are going to take away 4. They will go in our cup. We have 4 left. That will go in the small box. That is called the difference. It is the difference between what we had in the beginning and what we took away? **Teacher:** Let's try another one. Let's say I had 10. I took away 5. I put them in the cup. I have 5 left and those slide down to the little box. That is the difference between what we had and what we took away. **Teacher:** Now you all are each going to have your own subtraction machine. 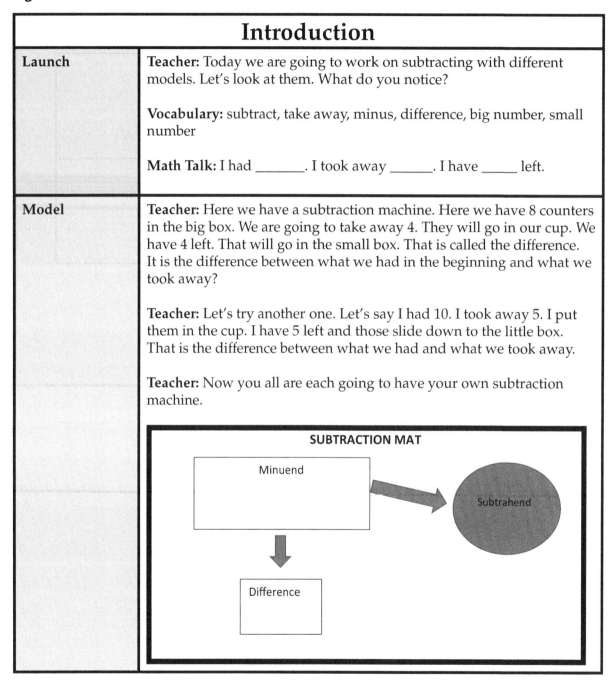

Checking for Understanding	The teacher passes out subtraction cards. Students pull a card and act out their problems. The students each get a chance to share their problem and explain how they solved it.
	Maria: I had 20. I took away 10. I have 10 left.

Math Talk: I had _____. I took away _____. I have _____ left.

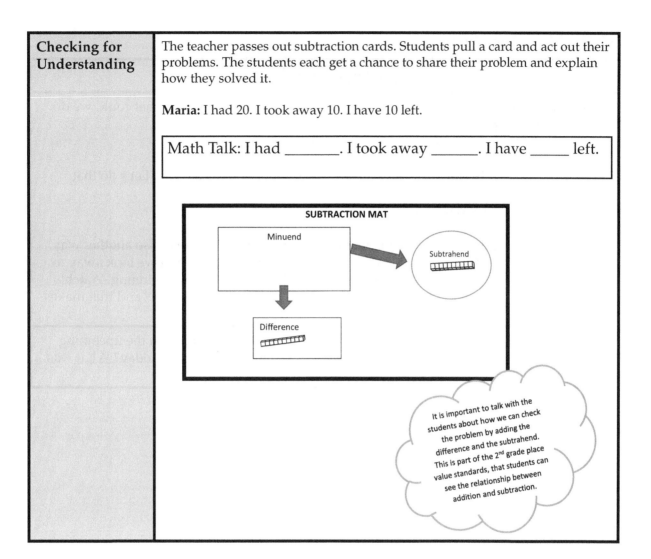

SUBTRACTION MAT

Minuend

Subtrahend

Difference

It is important to talk with the students about how we can check the problem by adding the difference and the subtrahend. This is part of the 2nd grade place value standards, that students can see the relationship between addition and subtraction.

Figure 5.51 Student Activity

Student Activity	
Guided Practice/ Checking for Understanding	**Teacher:** If we wanted to double-check the answer, what could we do? **Todd:** We could count on our fingers. **Teacher:** Yes, we could see if we get the same answer. Let's do that. **Marta:** We could use the number path. **Teacher:** Yes, let's do that. You know what? There is also another way to check. We could count our difference and the part we took away to see if we had the same amount that we had at the beginning. Watch. I could count 10 in the cup and 10 in the difference box and that makes 20. So I know that 20 take away 10 is 10.
Set Up for Independent Practice	**Teacher:** We are going to be talking more about this in the upcoming days. Are there any questions? What was interesting today? What was tricky?

Figure 5.52 Lesson Close

Close
♦ What did we do today? ♦ What was the math we were practicing? ♦ What were we doing with our number wands? ♦ Was this easy or tricky? ♦ Turn to a partner and state one thing you learned today.

Figure 5.53 Half Fact Cards

2 – 1	10 – 5
4 – 2	6 – 3
12 – 6	8 – 4
14 – 7	16 – 8
18 – 9	20 – 10

Figure 5.54 Subtraction Mat

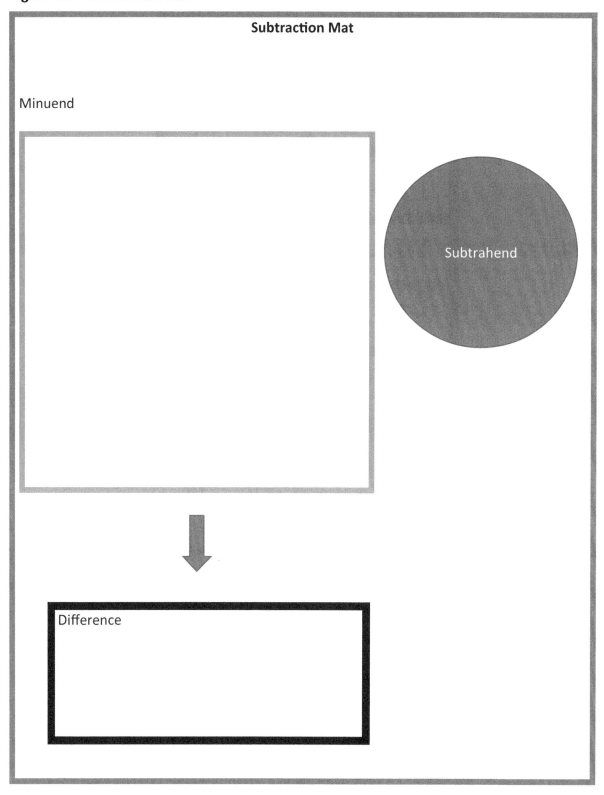

Pictorial Lesson

Figure 5.55 Pictorial Introduction

	Introduction
Launch	**Teacher:** Today we are going to continue to work on subtracting half facts with models. Let's review our vocabulary and our anchor chart. **Vocabulary:** subtract, take away, minus, difference, half facts, doubles **Teacher:** Who wants to talk about our vocabulary? **Sara:** Difference is the answer. **David:** Subtract means to take away. **Mike:** We use the minus sign in the number sentence to subtract.
Model	**Teacher:** Let's look at a card. Who can tell me a story about this card? **Amita:** There were 8 bananas. The kids ate 4. How many are left? **Tim:** 4. **Lin:** How do you know? **Tim:** Because 4 + 4 is 8 so 8 take away 4 is 4. **Chang:** I agree.
Checking for Understanding	**Teacher:** So this is what we are going to do today. You will get a card, tell a story, solve it, and then explain your strategy. Any questions? **Kane:** Let's go! I like stories!

Figure 5.56 Student Activity

Student Activity	
Guided Practice/ Checking for Understanding	**Teacher:** Who wants to go first? **Stephanie:** I do. There were 4 bananas. The kids ate 2. There are 2 left.  **Teacher:** How could we check it? **Melissa:** We could think 2 + 2 is 4. It's a doubles fact. **Todd:** Here is a problem. There were 8 orange slices. The kids ate 4. There are 4 left. 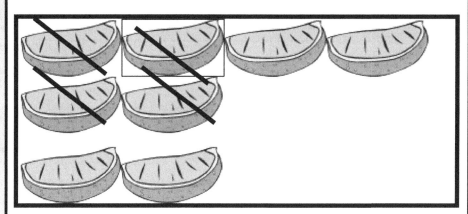 **Teacher:** How could we check it? **John:** We could add 4 + 4 and that makes 8. 8 take away 4 is 4 and 4 plus 4 is 8! **Marcus:** There were 10 juices. The kids drank 5. There were 5 left. So . . . 5 plus 5 is 10 and 10 take away 5 is 5. 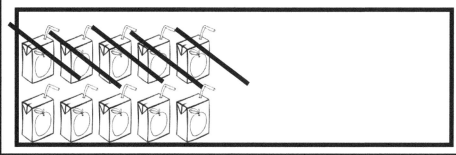
Set Up for Independent Practice	**Teacher:** We are going to be talking more about this in the upcoming days. Are there any questions? What was interesting today? What was tricky?

Figure 5.57 Lesson Close

Close
♦ What did we do today?
♦ What was the math we were practicing?
♦ Was this easy or tricky?
♦ Turn to a partner and state one thing you learned today.

Figure 5.58 Half Fact Cards

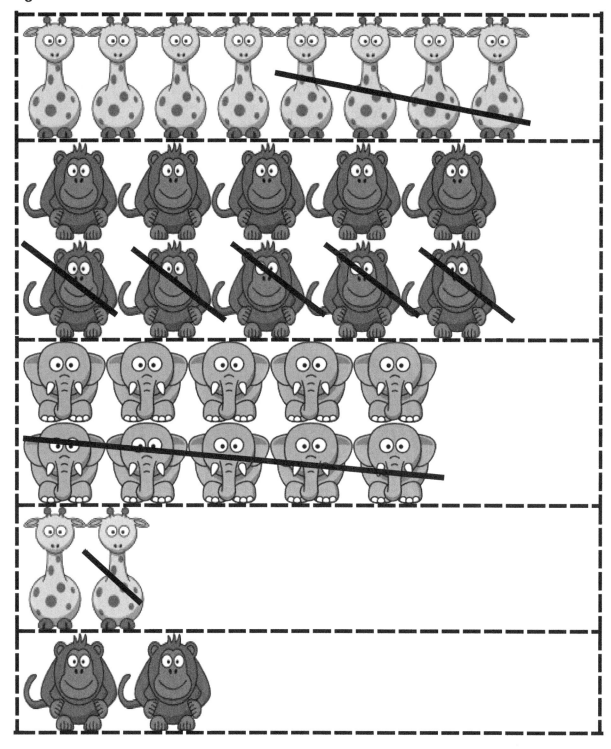

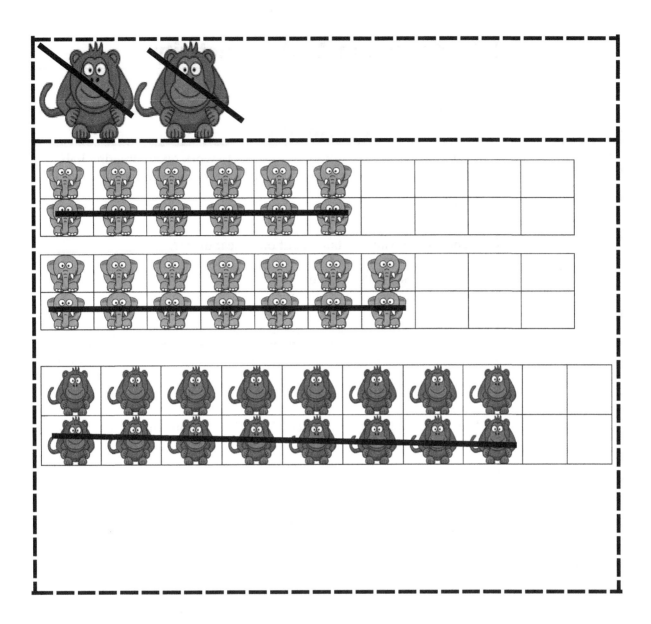

Introduction to Abstract Activity

Figure 5.59a Abstract Introduction

	Introduction
Launch	**Teacher:** Today we are going to continue to work on subtracting half facts with models. Let's review our vocabulary and our anchor chart. **Vocabulary:** subtract, take away, minus, difference, half facts, doubles, **Teacher:** Who wants to talk about our vocabulary? **Sara:** Difference is the answer **David:** Subtract means to take away **Mike:** We use the minus sign in the number sentence to subtract.
Model	**Teacher:** We are going to play half fact war. You will each pick a card. Whoever has the largest difference will win. Tim and Clara play a round. Who has the largest difference? **Clara:** I do. I have a difference of 7 and Tim has one of 5. I win both cards. $10 - 5$ $14 - 7$
Checking for Understanding	**Teacher:** So this is what we are going to do today. You will each get a deck and play war. Any questions? **Kane:** Let's go!

Abstract Lesson

Figure 5.59 Student Activity

Student Activity	
Guided Practice/ Checking for Understanding	The teacher listens as the students play the game. **Tom:** I have 12 – 6. **Mike:** I have 16 – 8. **Tom:** I have the smaller difference. I have a difference of 6 and he has a difference of 8.
Set Up for Independent Practice	**Teacher:** We are going to be talking more about this in the upcoming days. Are there any questions? What was interesting today? What was tricky?

Figure 5.60 Half Fact Flash Cards

2 – 1	10 – 5
4 – 2	6 – 3
12 – 6	8 – 4
14 – 7	16 – 8
18 – 9	20 – 10

Section Summary

Teaching subtraction is foundational. Students need to actually do many subtraction problems on different models, including the ten frame, rekenrek, and number lines. There should be an equal amount of time spent on subtraction strategies as on addition, and the connections between the two should constantly be made. The research says that subtraction is much more difficult for children than addition (Kamii, Kirkland, & Lewis, 2001, p. 33). It is important for students to master addition so that they can use that knowledge to help them with subtraction (Kamii et al., 2001). Make sure to build a strong foundation with concrete materials and drawings before rushing students to solve just abstract problems.

Depth of Knowledge

Depth of Knowledge (Figure 5.61) is a framework that encourages us to ask questions that require that students think, reason, explain, defend, and justify their thinking (Webb, 2002). Here is snapshot of what that can look like in terms of fluency work. It is important to think about what strategies you are working on with the students. In working in small groups on fluency, be sure to ask open questions so that students can think and reason out loud with others.

Figure 5.61 DOK Chart

	What are different strategies and models that we can use to explore bridging 10 when adding?	What are different strategies and models to explore subtracting back through ten?	What are different strategies and models that we can use to explore doubles plus 1 facts?	What are different strategies and models that we can use to explore subtraction half facts?
DOK Level 1 (These are questions where students are required to simply recall/reproduce an answer/do a procedure.)	$2 + 9$	$12 - 9$	$8 + 7$	$8 - 4$
DOK Level 2 (These are questions where students have to use information, think about concepts and reason.) This is considered a more challenging problem than a level 1 problem.	$8 + ? = 12$ ___ $+ 4 = 13$ What does it mean to use ten when counting larger numbers? Why should we use the bridge 10 strategy? Explain how to bridge 10 with this problem: $7 + 4$	Explain what bridging through ten means when you are subtracting? What is your strategy for solving $14 - 9$?	Fill in the doubles plus 1 facts. $15 =$ ___ $+ 8$ $11 = 5 +$ ___ Explain what a doubles plus 1 strategy means.	$10 -$ ___ $= 5$ ___ $- 6 = 6$ $14 -$ ___ $= 7$
DOK Level 3 (These are questions where students have to reason, plan, explain, justify, and defend their thinking.)	Give me an example of a bridge 10 fact when adding. Model $8 + 7$ in two different ways. Explain how you know your answer is correct.	Give me an example of using the bridge 10 strategy when subtracting. Model $13 - 5$ in two different ways. Explain how you know your answer is correct.	Is $5 + 2$ a doubles plus 1 fact? Why or why not. Explain your thinking and defend your answer.	Tell me a half fact subtraction story. Model and solve it. Explain how you know your answer is correct. How can knowing my doubles help me with my half facts?

Figure 5.62 Asking rigorous questions:

DOK 1	DOK 2	DOK 3
	At this level, students explain their thinking.	At this level, students have to justify, defend, and prove their thinking with objects, drawings, and diagrams.
What is the answer to . . . ? Can you model the problem? Can you identify the answer that matches this equation?	How do you know that the equation is correct? Can you pick the correct answer and explain why it is correct? How can you model that problem in more than one way? What is another way to model that problem? Can you model that on the . . . ? Give me an example of a . . . type of problem . . . Which answer is incorrect? Explain your thinking.	Can you prove that your answer is correct? Prove that . . . Explain why that is the answer. . . . Show me how to solve that and explain what you are doing. Defend your thinking.

Resources

A great resource for asking open questions is Marion Small's *Good Questions: Great Ways to Differentiate Mathematics Instruction in the Standards-Based Classroom* (2017). Also, Robert Kaplinsky has done a great job in pushing our thinking forward with the Depth of Knowledge Matrices he created (https://robertkaplinsky.com/depth-knowledge-matrix-elementary-math/). Another site for matrix: http://images.pcmac.org/Uploads/ConecuhCountyBOE/ConecuhCounty-BOE/Divisions/DocumentsCategories/Documents/Sample%20Mathematics.pdf (Kentucky Math Department, 2007)

Key Points

- ◆ Bridging Ten Facts for Addition
- ◆ Bridging Ten Facts for Subtraction
- ◆ Doubles Plus 1
- ◆ Subtraction Half Facts

Chapter Summary

It is essential that we work on basic fact fluency with students in small guided math groups. We have to take them through the cycle of concrete, pictorial, and abstract activities. We need to make sure that students understand, can explain, and appropriately use the various strategies. Just because the pacing calendar is working on a specific strategy, in no way implies that the students are actually ready to be working on that strategy. Therefore, it is essential that we pull groups and work with students in their zone of proximal development. We then follow this work up with workstations and homework that correlates with the concepts they are working on. Fluency is a continuum and all the students are working toward the grade-level fluency, but they are not all starting at the same point.

Reflection Questions

1. How are you currently teaching basic math fact fluency?
2. Are you making sure that you do concrete, pictorial, and abstract activities?
3. What do your students struggle with the most and what ideas are you taking away from this chapter that might inform your work around those struggles?

References

Baroody, A. J., Purpura, D. J., Eiland, M. D., Reid, E. E., & Paliwal, V. (2016). Does fostering reasoning strategies for relatively difficult basic combinations promote transfer by K-3 students? *Journal of Educational Psychology*, *108*(4), 576–591. https://doi.org/10.1037/edu0000067

Boaler, J. (2015). *Fluency without fear: Research evidence on the best ways to learn math facts*. Retrieved September 6, 2019, from www.youcubed.org/evidence/fluency-without-fear/

Brownell, W. A. (1956, October). Meaning and skill-maintaining the balance. *Arithmetic Teacher*, *3*, 129–136.

Brownell, W. A. (1956/1987). Meaning and skill: Maintaining the balance. *Arithmetic Teacher*, *34*(8), 18–25.

Brownell, W. A., & Chazal, C. B. (1935, September). The effects of premature drill in third-grade arithmetic. *Journal of Educational Research*, *29*, 17–28.

Godfrey, C., & Stone, J. (2013). Mastering fact fluency: Are they game? *Teaching Children Mathematics*, *20*(2), 96–101.

Henry, V., & Brown, R. (2008, March). First-grade basic facts: An investigation into teaching and learning of an accelerated, high-demand memorization standard. *Journal for Research in Mathematics Education*, *30*(2), 1153–1183.

Kamii, C., Kirkland, L., & Lewis, B. (2001). Fluency in subtraction compared with addition. *Journal of Mathematical Behavior*, *20*, 33–42.

Kilpatrick, J., Swafford, J., & Findell, B. (Eds.). (2001). *Adding it up: Helping children learn mathematics*. Washington, DC: National Academy Press, Mathematics Learning Study Committee, Center for Education, Division of Behavioral and Social Sciences and Education, National Research Council.

Kentucky Department of Education (2007). Support Materials for Core Content for Assessment Version 4.1 Mathematics. Retrieved from the internet on January 15th, 2017.

National Center for Education Evaluation and Regional Assistance. (2009). *Assisting students struggling with mathematics: Response to intervention (RtI) for elementary and middle schools,*

2009–4060. IES. Retrieved from http://ies.ed.gov/ncee; http://ies.ed.gov/ncee/wwc/publications/practiceguides/

National Council of Teachers of Mathematics. (2000). *Principles and standards for school mathematics*. Reston, VA: Author.

Newton, R. (2016). *Math running records*. New York: Routledge.

Newton, R., Record, A., & Mello, A. (2020). *Fluency doesn't just happen*. New York: Routledge.

Small, M. (2017). *Good questions: Great ways to differentiate mathematics instruction in the standards-based classroom* (3rd ed.). New York, NY: Teachers College Press.

Thornton, C. (1978). Emphasizing thinking strategies in basic fact instruction. *Journal for Research in Mathematics Education, 9*(3), 214–227.

Van de Walle, J. A. (2007). *Elementary and middle school mathematics: Teaching developmentally*. Boston: Pearson, Allyn and Bacon.

Webb, N. (2002). *An analysis of the alignment between mathematics standards and assessments for three states*. Paper presented at the annual meeting of the American educational Research Association, New Orleans, LA.

6

Small-Group Lessons for Developing Algebraic Thinking

When working on the big ideas of algebra in the primary grades, it is very important that students have a chance to reason about situations and numbers. Algebraic thinking must be developed from the beginning of school. In first grade, students are also playing around with the commutative and associative properties. These are fundamental building blocks to later algebraic work. Students must be given multiple opportunities to explore and discuss equations and their meanings with different types of manipulatives and drawings. In second grade, the work must continue around ideas of missing numbers and how to find them using various strategies. Also, students should continue to explore the relationships between addition and subtraction.

It is essential that students get to really think about equations and the meaning of the numbers and the equal sign. Students need opportunities to talk in small groups to discuss what is happening, to think about if they understand and agree with what is being said, and also to defend their own thinking and prove their ideas with manipulatives and drawings. So, as this work is being done in small groups, teachers should focus not only on the content but also on the practices.

In this chapter we will explore:

♦ Odd/Even Numbers
♦ Arrays
♦ Missing Numbers
♦ True/False Equations

Let's Talk About the Research!

Isler, Stephens, and Kang (2016) posit that in elementary school we need to develop the four algebraic thinking practices of generalizing, representing, justifying, and reasoning with mathematical relationships (Blanton, Levi, Crites, Dougherty, & Zbiek, 2011; Kaput, Carraher, & Blanton, 2008).

Research shows "that the use of pictorial models significantly improved the Algebraic thinking skills of the pupils. Interviews from the pupils revealed that pictorial models helped them to solve problems easier" (Tagle, Belecina, & Ocampo, 2016).

Math researchers have noted that students should be able to use a variety of representations to explain their thinking. The more ways they can use "visually, i.e. diagrams, pictures, or graphs; numerically, i.e. tables and lists; symbolically; and verbally," the better they can unpack the concepts. Each representation "contributes to the understanding of the ideas presented" (Tagle et al., 2016; see also Carpenter, Levi, Franke, & Zeringue, 2005; Blanton et al., 2019).

Blanton and Kaput (2003) argue that teachers must foster algebraic thinking in their classrooms by having "students modeling, exploring, arguing, predicting, conjecturing, and testing their ideas, as well as practicing computational skills."

Figure 6.1 Overview

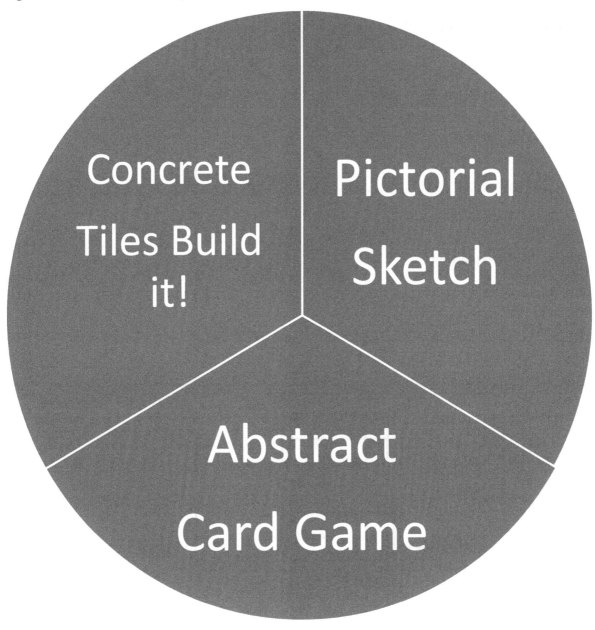

Exploring Even and Odd Numbers

Overview

Figure 6.2 Planning Template

Even or Odd		
Big Idea: Numbers can be even or odd.		**Materials**
Enduring Understanding: Students understand that even numbers can be paired and odd numbers cannot.		♦ Tools: Cubes
		♦ Templates: Ten Frame
Essential Question: How do we determine if a number is even or odd?		♦ Cards
I can statement: I can determine if numbers are even or odd.		♦ Crayons
Cycle of Engagement		
Concrete: Use Counters		
Pictorial: Draw It		
Abstract: Discuss Numbers 2 is even		
Levels of Understanding ♦ Novice ♦ Apprentice ♦ Practitioner ♦ Expert		
Even—Each 1 has a partner.	Odd—There isn't a partner for each giraffe.	
		Vocabulary & Language Frames ♦ Odd ♦ Even ♦ Partner ♦ Pair

Figure 6.3 Differentiation

Three Differentiated Lessons
In this series of lessons, students are working on the concept of *even and odd numbers*. They are developing this concept through concrete activities, pictorial activities, and abstract activities. Here are some things to think about as you do these lessons.

Emerging	On Grade Level	Above Grade Level
Students should do lots of explorations with the counters.	The standard is that students can state if a number is odd or even. After many explorations with manipulatives, have students focus on the pattern.	Work with larger numbers.

WATCH OUT Looking for Misunderstandings and Common Errors

Focus on students being able to prove it with smaller numbers and recognize the pattern. Work on this all year, by having students decide if the number of the date is odd or even by building out the month with cubes. Every day, the students can see and discuss if the number is odd or even (this is an idea from Math Their Way: Calendar Newsletter, 2021).

Concrete Lesson

Figure 6.4 Concrete Introduction

Introduction

I Can Statement: *I CAN explain about even and odd numbers.*

Launch	**Teacher:** Today we are going to talk about even and odd numbers. We have been looking at them in whole group. Remember we read the book *Even Steven and Odd Todd*. Today we are going to build the numbers to determine if they are even or odd. **Vocabulary:** even, odd, pair, sum **Math Talk:** _____ is even. I can prove it. _____ is odd. I can model it. Let's talk about 7. Who can explain this number?
Model	**Yessenia:** Ok . . . I am going to build it with the counters. So it is odd because one of them doesn't have a pair.
Checking for Understanding	**Teacher:** Who has a question for her? **Tyrone:** I do. Are you sure? Can you prove it another way? **Yessenia:** It doesn't have a pair and when it doesn't have a partner it is odd. Look at the anchor chart. 7 is under odd. **Teacher:** Ok, now I am going to give each one of you a number card and I want you to model your number and then talk about it. *The teacher passes out the cards.*

Figure 6.5 Student Activity

	Student Activity
Guided Practice/ Checking for Understanding	Students go around the table and each of them tells how they modeled their problem. **Veronica:** 6 is even because each counter has a partner. 6 is ____ because ____. **Mark:** Can you show another way? **Veronica:** Yes, I can prove it with drawings,
Set Up for Independent Practice	*Students continue sharing their work. Teacher wraps up by asking what is easy, what is tricky, and if there are any questions.*

Figure 6.6 Lesson Close

Close
◆ What did we do today? ◆ What was the math we were practicing? ◆ What are ways we were modeling our thinking? ◆ Was this easy or tricky? ◆ Turn to a partner and state one thing you learned today.

Pictorial Lesson

Figure 6.7 Pictorial Introduction

Introduction

I am learning about odd and even numbers.

Launch	**Teacher:** Today we are going to continue to work on proving whether a number is odd or even. (*Students should talk about what they did last time.*) **Vocabulary:** even, odd, pair, sum **Math Talk:** _____ is even. I can prove it. _____ is odd. I can model it.
Model	**Teacher:** Today we are going to record our thinking with sketches and other models. Who wants to go first? **Taylor:** **Timmy:** Who can prove it another way? **Marta:** I can show it on my fingers! (*She giggles and crosses all her fingers and then her thumbs*) See, every finger has a partner. *The students giggle and try Marta's way.*
Checking for Understanding	**Teacher:** Yes. Did everyone notice how she drew a picture to model her thinking? We can do it by drawings or with other models such as the rekenrek or the number bracelets.

Figure 6.8 Student Activity

Student Activity	
Kate: I had 8 and I proved that it is even because each one has a partner.	
Guided Practice/ Checking for Understanding	**Teacher:** Ok, now you all are going to try more modeling. I am going to pass around a problem to each person and you will model it and then share your thinking. 8 is _____ because _____. **Teacher:** Yes. This is a great. (*Students go around and everyone shows their work and shares their thinking.*)
Set Up for Independent Practice	**Teacher:** Who wants to talk about what we practiced today? **Brian:** We talked about even and odd numbers. **Marta:** We talked about how to model it so you can prove if it is even or odd. **Teacher:** We are going to continue to talk about even and odd numbers. I want you to play around with bigger numbers and then we are going to talk about how you know if a number is even or odd. You may go to your next workstation now.

Figure 6.9 Lesson Close

Close
♦ What did we do today?   ♦ What was the math we were practicing?   ♦ Was this easy or tricky?   ♦ Turn to a partner and state one thing you learned today.

Figure 6.10 Prove That Cards

Prove that:	Prove that:
1 is ____ because ___.	2 is ____ because ___.

Prove that:	Prove that:
3 is ____ because ___.	4 is ____ because ___.

Prove that:	Prove that:
5 is ____ because ___.	**6 is ____ because ___.**

Prove that:	Prove that:
7 is ____ because ___.	**8 is ____ because ___.**

Prove that:	Prove that:
9 is ____ because ___.	**10 is ____ because ___.**

Prove that:

11 is _____ because _____.

Prove that:

12 is _____ because _____.

Prove that:

13 is _____ because _____.

Prove that:

14 is _____ because _____.

Prove that:

15 is _____ because _____.

Prove that:

16 is _____ because _____.

Prove that:

17 is _____ because _____.

Prove that:

18 is _____ because _____.

Prove that:

19 is _____ because _____.

Prove that:

20 is _____ because _____.

Abstract Lesson

Figure 6.11 Abstract Introduction

	Introduction
Launch	**Teacher:** Today we are going to continue to work on odd and even numbers. We are going to play a card game. Let's review our vocabulary and our anchor chart. **Vocabulary:** odd, even, partners, pairs **Math Talk:** *I am playing for even numbers.* *I am playing for odd numbers.* *This number is even because. . .* *This number is odd because. . .* **Teacher:** Ok, to play the game, you roll the dice to see who goes first. The bigger number is odd and the smaller number is even. The smaller number goes first. You take turns pulling a card from the deck. If it is even and you are even, you can keep it. If not, you put it at the end of the deck. Keep pulling and the first person to get 10 cards first wins. Let's practice.
Model	**Teacher:** Let's try one. Mike pulled a 7 but he is playing for the even cards. Can he keep this card? **Marta:** No because 7 is an odd number. He puts it back at the bottom of the pile. **Kellie:** I pulled an 8 and I am playing for even numbers. I get to keep my card.
Checking for Understanding	**Teacher:** Ok, does everybody understand how to play? Ok, you are going to play with your math partners. Don't forget to shuffle the deck.

Figure 6.12 Student Activity

Student Activity	
Guided Practice/ Checking for Understanding	As the students play the game, the teacher listens, asks questions, and takes notes. **Larry:** I am odd. I pulled a 15. I get to keep it. **Trina:** I am even. I pulled a 12. I get to keep it. **Larry:** I pulled 6 so I put it back because it is even. **Teacher:** Can you prove it? **Larry:** See, he puts up his fingers and finds a partner for every finger. Students continue to play the game and teacher takes notes.
Set Up for Independent Practice	**Teacher:** Ok, I have a question for you all. How would I know that 17 is odd without having to prove it? **Carl:** 7 is odd so 17 would be odd. Like 17 is 10 and 7 so with the 10 everybody has a partner but with the 7 they don't. **Teacher:** Wow! Great thinking and great explanation. I want you all to be thinking about how we know if a number is odd or even by looking at the numerals in that number. Explore that, and next time we meet we will play this game with higher numbers and think about which numbers are odd and which ones are even. You all can go to the rug because we are about to do the share.

Figure 6.13 Lesson Close

Close
◆ What did we do today? ◆ What was the math we were practicing? ◆ Was this easy or tricky? ◆ Turn to a partner and state one thing you learned today.

Figure 6.14 Cards

1	2	3	4
5	6	7	8
9	10	11	12
13	14	15	16
17	18	19	20
21	22	23	24
27	38	49	50
91	62	73	100
39	28	67	80
92	65	71	90

Section Summary

Even and odd numbers are fun for students. In this section we discussed ideas of how to build their understanding beyond just saying a poem. Although I think the poems are a nice addition, they shouldn't be the core of the teaching. Make sure that students can explain their thinking and discuss the pattern. In your even and odd toolkit, you should have counters, hundred grids, and picture books or videos (digital toolkit). The classic book *Even Steven and Odd Todd* by Katheryn Cristaldi (1996) is a great anchor for a mini-unit on this topic.

Overview

Figure 6.15 Overview

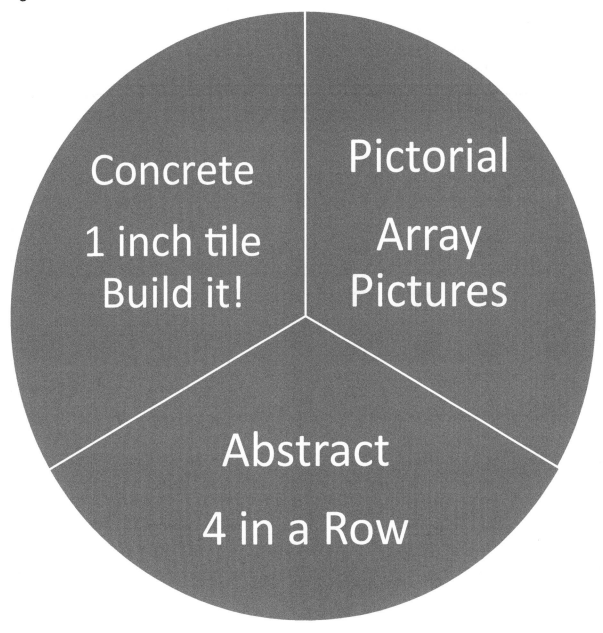

Figure 6.16 Planning Template

Arrays	
Big Idea: Arrays can be formed to quickly count. **Enduring Understanding:** We can arrange the same number of counters in different ways. **Essential Question:** Why do we make arrays? Where do we see them in real life? **I can statement:** I can make and count arrays.	**Materials** ◆ Tools: Cubes ◆ Templates: Ten Frames ◆ Cards ◆ Crayons
An array is a group of objects arranged into columns and rows. Column Row	**Concrete** **Pictorial:** **Abstract:** $3 + 3 + 3$ **Vocabulary & Language Frames** ◆ Group ◆ Addends ◆ Sum ◆ Array ___ and ___ and ____ make _____ The sum of ___ and ____ and ____ is _____.

Figure 6.17 Differentiation

Three Differentiated Lessons		
In this series of lessons, students are working on the concept of *arrays*. They are developing this concept through concrete activities, pictorial activities, and abstract activities. Here are some things to think about as you do these lessons.		
Emerging	**On Grade Level**	**Above Grade Level**
Do a lot of work with students building the arrays with different manipulatives.	The standard is that students can build up to a 5 by 5 array in many states.	Work with larger numbers.
Looking for Misunderstandings and Common Errors		
Students have trouble building and describing the array. There is a great Twitter community hashtag about arrays. They have really interesting ones for students to discuss: #arraychat		

Concrete Lesson

Figure 6.18 Concrete Introduction

	Introduction
Launch	**Teacher:** Today we are going to talk about arrays. We are going to make them. Remember we were making people arrays in whole group. Today we are going to make them with our tiles. **Vocabulary:** addends, grouping numbers, sum, total, equals, same as, arrays **Math Talk:** This is an array. It is ____ by _____. Another way to do it is ____ by ____.
Model	**Teacher:** I have the number 8. Who can show me a way to arrange these counters in an array? **Shirley:** I did 4 groups of 2. My equation is 2 + 2 + 2 + 2.
Checking for Understanding	**Teacher:** Is there another way to do it? **Trevor:** I did 2 groups of 4. 4 + 4. **Teacher:** Ok, now I am going to give each one of you a card and I want you to model an array and then talk about it. (*The teacher passes out the problems.*)

Figure 6.19 Student Activity

	Student Activity
Guided Practice/Checking for Understanding	Students go around the table and each of them tells how they modeled their array.

Vivi: I got a 10. I did 5 groups of 2.

■ ■

■ ■

■ ■

■ ■

■ ■

Teacher: Von, what question could you ask Vivi?
Von: Is there another way you could do it?
Vivi: I could do 2 groups of 5.

■ ■ ■ ■ ■
■ ■ ■ ■ ■

Von: I got a 6. I made an array of 3 and 3.

■ ■ ■
■ ■ ■

Vivi: Is there another way to show it?
Von: I could do 3 rows of 2.

■ ■
■ ■
■ ■ |
| **Set Up for Independent Practice** | **Teacher:** Ok, let's wrap up. What were we studying today? How do we use arrays in real life? What is easy or tricky? Are there any questions or comments? |

Figure 6.20 Lesson Close

Close
♦ What did we do today? ♦ What was the math we were practicing? ♦ What are ways we were modeling our thinking? ♦ Was this easy or tricky? ♦ Turn to a partner and state one thing you learned today.

Figure 6.21 Cards

2	4	5	8	10
12	14	16	18	20
3	6	9	15	24

Pictorial Lesson

Figure 6.22 Pictorial Introduction

	Introduction
Launch	**Teacher:** Today we are going to talk about arrays. We are going to describe them. Remember we were making people arrays in whole group. Today we are going to look at pictures. **Vocabulary:** addends, grouping numbers, sum, total, equals, same as, arrays **Math Talk:** This is an array. It is ____ by ____. Another way to do it is ____ by ____.
Model	**Teacher:** Today we are going to continue to work on arrays. I am going to show you a picture of an array and I want you to describe it and write the equation. Who wants to describe this picture? **Tony:** It is eggs. It is 2 groups of 5. **Teacher:** Great. Does anybody see this array a different way?
Checking for Understanding	**Teacher:** Great. Does anybody see this array a different way? **Lucy:** Yes, it could be 5 groups of 2. 2 + 2 + 2 + 2 + 2. **Teacher:** Ok, now you all are going to try it. I am going to pass around an array card to each person and you will model it and then share your thinking.

Figure 6.23 Student Activity

Student Activity	
Guided Practice/Checking for Understanding	The students go around and explain their card. **Kate:** I had 3 rows and 3 columns. I had 8 altogether. It is $3 + 3 + 3$. **Tami:** Are you sure that is 8? **Kate:** I mean 9.
	Equation:
Set Up for Independent Practice	*Students go around and everyone shows their work and shares their thinking.*

Figure 6.24 Lesson Close

Close
♦ What did we do today? ♦ What was the math we were practicing? ♦ Was this easy or tricky? ♦ Turn to a partner and state one thing you learned today.

Figure 6.25 Cards

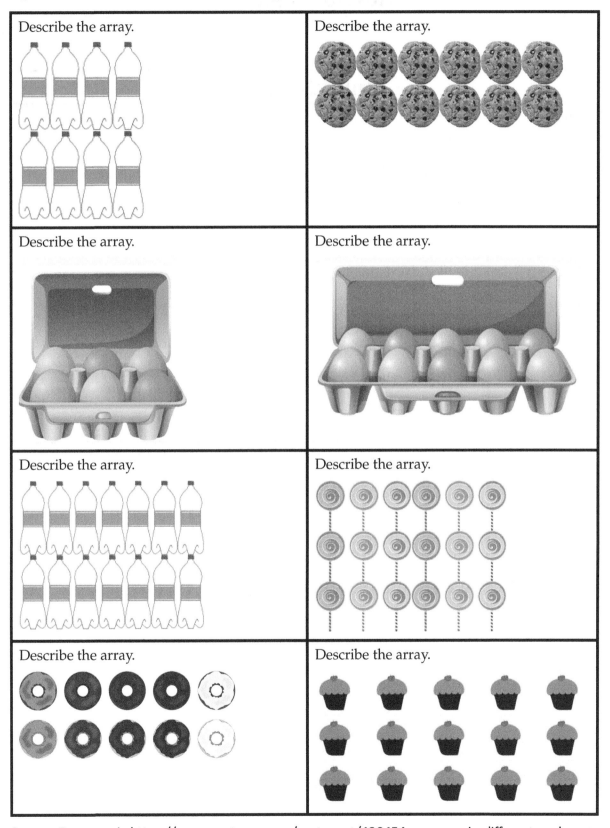

Describe the array.

Describe the array.

Describe the array.

Describe the array.

Describe the array.

Describe the array.

Describe the array.

Describe the array.

Source: Eggs are via https://www.vecteezy.com/vector-art/430454-raw-eggs-in-different-packages

Figure 6.26 Abstract Introduction

Introduction	
Launch	**Teacher:** Today we are going to continue to work on arrays. We are going to play a board game. Let's review our vocabulary and our anchor chart. **Vocabulary:** addends, grouping numbers, sum, total, equals, same as, arrays **Math Talk:** This is an array. It is ____ by ____. Another way to do it is ____ by ____. **Teacher:** Who wants to talk about our vocabulary? **Sara:** Arrays are groups of objects in a specific order. **David:** Columns go up and go down. **Mike:** Rows go across.
Model	**Teacher:** Today we are going to play array bump it.

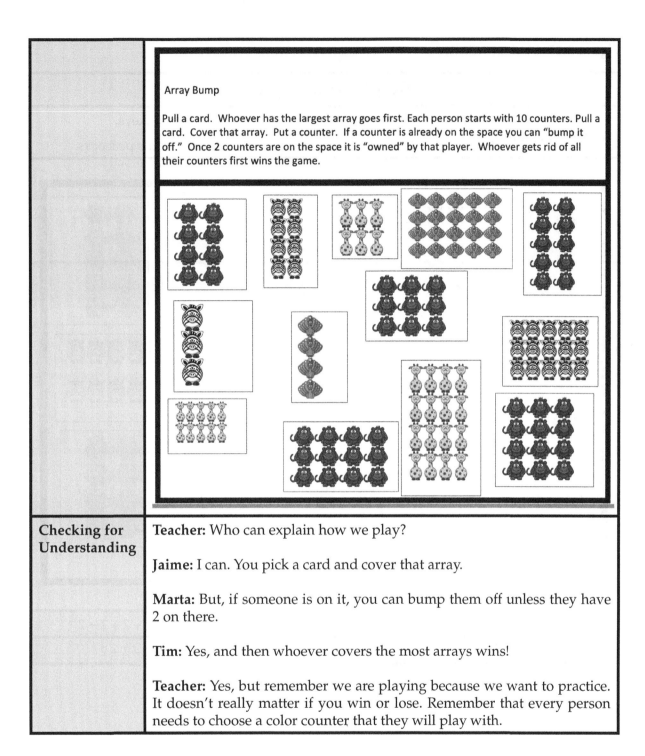

Array Bump

Pull a card. Whoever has the largest array goes first. Each person starts with 10 counters. Pull a card. Cover that array. Put a counter. If a counter is already on the space you can "bump it off." Once 2 counters are on the space it is "owned" by that player. Whoever gets rid of all their counters first wins the game.

Checking for Understanding	**Teacher:** Who can explain how we play? **Jaime:** I can. You pick a card and cover that array. **Marta:** But, if someone is on it, you can bump them off unless they have 2 on there. **Tim:** Yes, and then whoever covers the most arrays wins! **Teacher:** Yes, but remember we are playing because we want to practice. It doesn't really matter if you win or lose. Remember that every person needs to choose a color counter that they will play with.

Figure 6.27 Student Activity

Student Activity	
Guided Practice/Checking for Understanding	**Sue:** I picked 3 + 3 + 3. I covered the monkeys. **Brit:** I picked 1 + 1 + 1 and so I covered the peacocks.

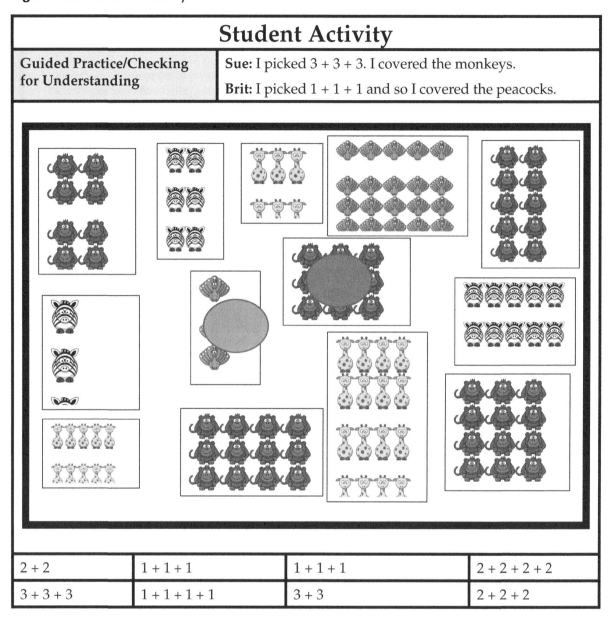

2 + 2	1 + 1 + 1	1 + 1 + 1	2 + 2 + 2 + 2
3 + 3 + 3	1 + 1 + 1 + 1	3 + 3	2 + 2 + 2

4 + 4 + 4 + 4	5 + 5 + 5	4 + 4 + 4	3 + 3 + 3 + 3
5 + 5 + 5 + 5	cover an array with more than 3 rows	cover an array with less than 3 columns	cover an array and name it

2 groups of 2	3 groups of 1	2 groups of 5
4 groups of 2	3 groups of 3	4 groups of 1
2 groups of 3	3 groups of 2	4 groups of 4
3 groups of 5	3 groups of 4	4 groups of 3
4 groups of 5		

Figure 6.28 Lesson Close

Close

♦ What did we do today?
♦ What was the math we were practicing?
♦ Was this easy or tricky?
♦ Turn to a partner and state one thing you learned today.

Figure 6.29 Cards

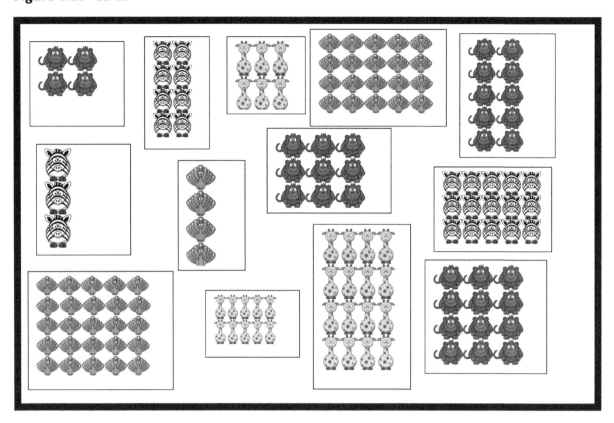

Figure 6.30 Cards

2 + 2	1 + 1 + 1	5 + 5	2 + 2 + 2 + 2
3 + 3 + 3	1 + 1 + 1 + 1	3 + 3	2 + 2 + 2
4 + 4 + 4 + 4	5 + 5 + 5	4 + 4 + 4	3 + 3 + 3 + 3
5 + 5 + 5 + 5	cover an array with more than 3 rows	cover an array with less than 3 columns	cover an array and name it

Figure 6.31 Cards

2 groups of 2	3 groups of 1	2 groups of 5
4 groups of 2	3 groups of 3	4 groups of 1
2 groups of 3	3 groups of 2	4 groups of 4
3 groups of 5	3 groups of 4	4 groups of 3
4 groups of 5		

Section Summary

Teaching arrays is important. This is a foundation for students understanding multiplication. At the end of the year, work on this. Do it by having students build arrays with different manipulatives and then draw them. They should also look at arrays in real life and discuss not only the how but also the why. They should understand that arrays are a fast way to count. It is important that they understand the repeated addition that is the equation that names the array.

Figure 6.32 The Equal Sign

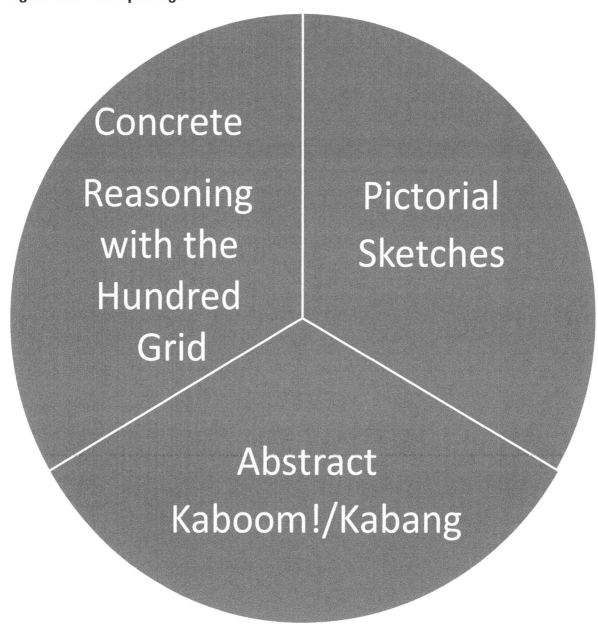

Figure 6.33 Planning Template

Missing Numbers	
Big Idea: Operation Meanings and Relationships **Enduring Understanding:** Students will understand that there are different strategies for finding the missing number. **Essential Question:** How do we determine missing numbers? **I can statement:** I can find missing numbers in equations.	**Materials** ♦ Tools: Cubes ♦ Templates: Ten Frame ♦ Cards ♦ Crayons
Cycle of Engagement **Concrete: Use Counters** **Pictorial** **Abstract** $5 + ? = 7$ $5 + 2 = 7$	**Vocabulary & Language Frames** ♦ Group ♦ Addends ♦ Sum ♦ Missing Numbers ___ and ___ and ____ make _____ The sum of ___ and ____ and ___ is _____.

Figure 6.34 Differentiation

Three Differentiated Lessons		
In this series of lessons, students are working on the concept of the missing number. They are developing this concept through concrete activities, pictorial activities, and abstract activities. Everybody should do the cycle. Some students progress through it more quickly than others. Here are some things to think about as you do these lessons.		
Emerging	**On Grade Level**	**Above Grade Level**
This is a first-grade standard and students are working on numbers within 20. As you introduce this to students, do a lot of work by acting it out and then doing it with manipulatives. Be sure to have students draw what they acted out and connect it to number models.	The concept is extended into second grade with numbers through 100. Students should be able to model it and explain it. So do lots of this work where students are modeling it and explaining it.	Once they have the concept, play lots of abstract games, including card games, board games, and dice games.

 # Looking for Misunderstandings and Common Errors

It is important to do many different explorations with finding the missing number. You want students to be able to reason about numbers and not just give instant answers from what they visually see. They should always be asked to explain their thinking, defend their answer with numbers, words, and pictures, and prove their thinking. Students have so much trouble with the equal sign. They often just think it means to put the answer. In this series of lessons, the focus is on students unpacking the equations and reasoning about them.

Figure 6.35 Concrete Introduction

Concrete and/or Visual Lesson

	Introduction
Launch	**Teacher:** Today we are going to talk about "missing numbers." **Vocabulary:** addends, missing numbers, sum, total, equals, same as **Math Talk:** This is the missing number.
Model	**Teacher:** How might we find missing numbers in a number sentence (equation)? Think about how we can prove things. Here is our anchor chart of ways we prove things.

Model (cont.)	**Teacher:** Let's look at this problem. The mermaid had 10 jewels. An octopus swam by and took some. Now there are only 5 left. How many did the octopus take? **Tracie:** 5. **Teacher:** How do you know? **Tracie:** Because 5 and 5 make 10.
Checking for Understanding	**Teacher:** Ok, let's see. What about if she had 50 and then the octopus took some? Now she only has 20 left. How many did the octopus take? **Carl:** 30 because 30 and 20 make 50. **Teacher:** Ok, now I am going to give each of you some jewels so that you can tell the story.

Figure 6.36 Student Activity

	Student Activity
Guided Practice/ Checking for Understanding	Students go around the table and each of them tells and models a word problem with a missing addend. They use place value blocks, hundred grids and rekenreks.

Verna: There was a mermaid. She had 44 jewels. The whale came and took some. Now she only has 39 left. How many did he take? I can count up from 39 to 44. That is 5.

Teacher: Verna, what does the number sentence look like for your story?

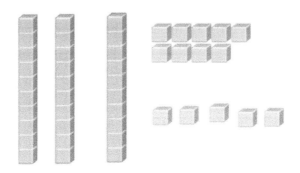

Verna: 44 − ? = 39.

Teacher: Who wants to share another story?

Todd: There was a pirate that had 100 jewels. The octopus came by and took some. Now he has 50 left. How many did the octopus take? |

	Marta: He took 50 because 50 and 50 make 100.
	Teacher: Todd, what does the number sentence look like for your story?
	Todd: $100 - ? = 50$.
	Teacher: Who has a question for Todd?
	Jamal: What is a strategy for solving your story?
	Todd: I could count up or count back. Either way it is 50. $50 + 50$ is 100.
Set Up for Independent Practice	**Teacher:** So, you all are using your number facts to find the missing number. Sometimes you are counting up. So we see that the equation that models the problem can actually be solved different ways. As we wrap up, who can explain what we did today?
	John: We looked at problems where you have something and then you take something away. You have to find the missing number.
	Teacher: What was easy, what was tricky? Are there any questions or comments?
	Taylor: I think finding the missing number is tricky sometimes when you have like $47 - ? = 29$.
	Teacher: Ok, so what is a way to think about that?
	Taylor: I like to use the hundred grid and count back.
	Teacher: Yes. That works! There are many ways to think about the problems. What is another strategy?
	Jamal: I like to count up.
	Teacher: We are going to continue to work on this in the upcoming days. You can go to your workstations.

Figure 6.37 Lesson Close

Close
♦ What did we do today?
♦ What was the math we were practicing?
♦ What are ways we were modeling our thinking?
♦ Was this easy or tricky?
♦ Turn to a partner and state one thing you learned today.

Figure 6.38 Storytelling Cards

The fruit stand had 30 boxes of strawberries. It sold some. Now it has 20. How many did it sell?

1	2	3	4	5	6	7	8	9	10
11	12	13	14	15	16	17	18	19	20
21	22	23	24	25	26	27	28	29	30
31	32	33	34	35	36	37	38	39	40
41	42	43	44	45	46	47	48	49	50
51	52	53	54	55	56	57	58	59	60
61	62	63	64	65	66	67	68	69	70
71	72	73	74	75	76	77	78	79	80
81	82	83	84	85	86	87	88	89	90
91	92	93	94	95	96	97	98	99	100

The fruit stand had 70 bags of apples. It sold some. Now it has 20. How many did it sell?

1	2	3	4	5	6	7	8	9	10
11	12	13	14	15	16	17	18	19	20
21	22	23	24	25	26	27	28	29	30
31	32	33	34	35	36	37	38	39	40
41	42	43	44	45	46	47	48	49	50
51	52	53	54	55	56	57	58	59	60
61	62	63	64	65	66	67	68	69	70
71	72	73	74	75	76	77	78	79	80
81	82	83	84	85	86	87	88	89	90
91	92	93	94	95	96	97	98	99	100

The fruit stand had 100 bags of bananas. It sold some. Now it has 50. How many did it sell?

1	2	3	4	5	6	7	8	9	10
11	12	13	14	15	16	17	18	19	20
21	22	23	24	25	26	27	28	29	30
31	32	33	34	35	36	37	38	39	40
41	42	43	44	45	46	47	48	49	50
51	52	53	54	55	56	57	58	59	60
61	62	63	64	65	66	67	68	69	70
71	72	73	74	75	76	77	78	79	80
81	82	83	84	85	86	87	88	89	90
91	92	93	94	95	96	97	98	99	100

The fruit stand had 45 bags of cherries. It sold some. Now it has 15. How many did it sell?

1	2	3	4	5	6	7	8	9	10
11	12	13	14	15	16	17	18	19	20
21	22	23	24	25	26	27	28	29	30
31	32	33	34	35	36	37	38	39	40
41	42	43	44	45	46	47	48	49	50
51	52	53	54	55	56	57	58	59	60
61	62	63	64	65	66	67	68	69	70
71	72	73	74	75	76	77	78	79	80
81	82	83	84	85	86	87	88	89	90
91	92	93	94	95	96	97	98	99	100

The bakery had 55 pies. It sold some. Now it has 20. How many did it sell?

1	2	3	4	5	6	7	8	9	10
11	12	13	14	15	16	17	18	19	20
21	22	23	24	25	26	27	28	29	30
31	32	33	34	35	36	37	38	39	40
41	42	43	44	45	46	47	48	49	50
51	52	53	54	55	56	57	58	59	60
61	62	63	64	65	66	67	68	69	70
71	72	73	74	75	76	77	78	79	80
81	82	83	84	85	86	87	88	89	90
91	92	93	94	95	96	97	98	99	100

The bakery had ___ cookies. It sold some. Now it has ___. How many did it sell?

1	2	3	4	5	6	7	8	9	10
11	12	13	14	15	16	17	18	19	20
21	22	23	24	25	26	27	28	29	30
31	32	33	34	35	36	37	38	39	40
41	42	43	44	45	46	47	48	49	50
51	52	53	54	55	56	57	58	59	60
61	62	63	64	65	66	67	68	69	70
71	72	73	74	75	76	77	78	79	80
81	82	83	84	85	86	87	88	89	90
91	92	93	94	95	96	97	98	99	100

The bakery had 90 cupcakes. It sold some. Now it has 40. How many did it sell?

1	2	3	4	5	6	7	8	9	10
11	12	13	14	15	16	17	18	19	20
21	22	23	24	25	26	27	28	29	30
31	32	33	34	35	36	37	38	39	40
41	42	43	44	45	46	47	48	49	50
51	52	53	54	55	56	57	58	59	60
61	62	63	64	65	66	67	68	69	70
71	72	73	74	75	76	77	78	79	80
81	82	83	84	85	86	87	88	89	90
91	92	93	94	95	96	97	98	99	100

The bakery had ___ cakes. It sold some. Now it has ___. How many did it sell?

1	2	3	4	5	6	7	8	9	10
11	12	13	14	15	16	17	18	19	20
21	22	23	24	25	26	27	28	29	30
31	32	33	34	35	36	37	38	39	40
41	42	43	44	45	46	47	48	49	50
51	52	53	54	55	56	57	58	59	60
61	62	63	64	65	66	67	68	69	70
71	72	73	74	75	76	77	78	79	80
81	82	83	84	85	86	87	88	89	90
91	92	93	94	95	96	97	98	99	100

The shoe store had 50 pairs of sandals. It sold some. Now it has 30. How many did it sell?

1	2	3	4	5	6	7	8	9	10
11	12	13	14	15	16	17	18	19	20
21	22	23	24	25	26	27	28	29	30
31	32	33	34	35	36	37	38	39	40
41	42	43	44	45	46	47	48	49	50
51	52	53	54	55	56	57	58	59	60
61	62	63	64	65	66	67	68	69	70
71	72	73	74	75	76	77	78	79	80
81	82	83	84	85	86	87	88	89	90
91	92	93	94	95	96	97	98	99	100

The shoe store had ___ pairs of sneakers. It sold some. Now it has ___. How many did it sell?

1	2	3	4	5	6	7	8	9	10
11	12	13	14	15	16	17	18	19	20
21	22	23	24	25	26	27	28	29	30
31	32	33	34	35	36	37	38	39	40
41	42	43	44	45	46	47	48	49	50
51	52	53	54	55	56	57	58	59	60
61	62	63	64	65	66	67	68	69	70
71	72	73	74	75	76	77	78	79	80
81	82	83	84	85	86	87	88	89	90
91	92	93	94	95	96	97	98	99	100

Pictorial Lesson

Figure 6.39 Pictorial Introduction

<table>
<tr><td colspan="2" align="center"><h2>Introduction</h2></td></tr>
<tr>
<td>Launch</td>
<td>

Teacher: Today we are going to continue to work on finding the missing number. (*Students should talk about what they did last time.*)

Vocabulary: addends, missing numbers, sum, total, equals, same as

Math Talk: This is the missing number.

</td>
</tr>
<tr>
<td>Model</td>
<td>

Teacher: Today we are going to record our thinking with sketches.

$55 - ? = 25$

Teacher: How could we solve this problem with math sketches?

Lucy: I know. You have to draw the 55 and then cross out until you only have 25 left. So the missing number is 30.

Teacher: How do we know that is correct?

Lucy: Because the 30 + 25 makes 55.

Teacher: Ok, so we can check the subtraction by addition?

</td>
</tr>
<tr>
<td>Checking for Understanding</td>
<td>

Teacher: Yes. Did you notice how she drew a picture to model her thinking? We can do it by drawing. Ok, now you all are going to try it. I am going to pass around a problem to each person and you will model it and then share your thinking.

</td>
</tr>
</table>

Figure 6.40 Student Activity

	Student Pictorial Activity
Guided Practice/ Checking for Understanding	**Kate:** I had 48 – ? = 25. I drew 48 and then I crossed out 23 so I had 25 left.
	$$48 - ? = 25$$
	HII 00000⌀⌀⌀
	How many did you draw? 48
	How many did you cross out? 25
	What is the missing addend? 23
	Teacher: Yes. This is great. I have one more question. What is a strategy for solving this problem?
	Maria: You could take away 20 and then take away 3 more to get to 25.
	Teacher: This is brilliant thinking! How does that sound? Show us.
	Ted: I took away 25. . . so I did 20 and the got 28 and then 5 more is 23 . . . and I know that 23 and 25 make 48 so that's the answer.
Set Up for Independent Practice	*Students go around and everyone shows their work and shares their thinking.*

Figure 6.41 Lesson Close

Close
◆ What did we do today?   ◆ What was the math we were practicing?   ◆ Was this easy or tricky?   ◆ Turn to a partner and state one thing you learned today.

Figure 6.42 Cards

Find the Missing Number $$47 - \, ? = 22$$ How many did you draw? How many did you cross out? What is the missing addend?	Find the Missing Number $$68 - \, ? = 54$$ How many did you draw? How many did you cross out? What is the missing addend?
Find the Missing Number $$100 - \, ? = 25$$ How many did you draw? How many did you cross out? What is the missing addend?	Find the Missing Number $$50 - \, ? = 20$$ How many did you draw? How many did you cross out? What is the missing addend?
Find the Missing Number $$75 - \, ? = 50$$ How many did you draw? How many did you cross out? What is the missing addend?	Find the Missing Number $$88 - \, ? = 28$$ How many did you draw? How many did you cross out? What is the missing addend?

Abstract Lesson

Figure 6.43 Abstract Introduction

	Introduction
Launch	**Teacher:** Today we are going to continue to work on finding the missing number. (*Students should talk about what they did last time.*) **Vocabulary:** addends, missing numbers, sum, total, equals, same as **Math Talk:** This is the missing number.
Model	**Teacher:** Today we are going to continue to work on missing numbers. It is Missing Number Kaboom! It is like regular Kaboom/Kabang—but . . . the popsicle sticks have missing numbers. On each popsicle stick is a missing number problem. We have a cup that has a variety of missing number problems. You and your partner take turns pulling a stick. You get to keep the stick if you get the answer correct. If you pull Kaboom you have to put all your sticks back in the bucket. But, if you get a Kabang you get to choose three sticks and solve them. After each person has had seven turns, the game is over. Whoever has the most sticks wins! **Vocabulary:** missing number, addend, sum, total
Checking for Understanding	**Teacher:** Who can explain what we are going to do? **Todd:** We are going to play Kaboom but today it is going to be about missing numbers. **Teacher:** Anybody have any questions? **Yessenia:** Wait, what? **Tami:** We are playing Kaboom, you know when you pick a stick but it might say Kaboom and then you lose all your sticks or it says Kabang and you can get more points if you get the answers right. **Yessenia:** Oh yeahhhhh. **Teacher:** Ok, let's play.

Figure 6.44 Student Activity

	Student Activity
Guided Practice/ Checking for Understanding	Students play the game with a partner. The teacher watches, comments, and asks questions. **Katie:** I pulled 88 – ? = 42. I counted up 8 to get to 50 and then 38 more to get to 88. 38 and 8 make 46. 46 and 42 make 88. So I'm right! **Nick:** 71 – ? = 16. I added 4 to each number to make an easier problem. I got 75 – 20 which is 55. 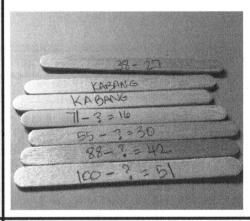
Set Up for Independent Practice	*Students continue the game and explaining their thinking. The teacher watches and takes notes. The popsicle sticks are differentiated by number ranges. After a bit, the teacher pulls everybody back together and asks them about the math they were doing. Students talk about what was easy and what was tricky. Then, they go and work in their workstations.*

Figure 6.45 Lesson Close

Close
♦ What did we do today? ♦ What was the math we were practicing? ♦ Was this easy or tricky? ♦ Turn to a partner and state one thing you learned today.

Figure 6.46 Cards

27 – ? = 13	17 – ? = 2	33 – ? = 28	40 – ? = 30
98 – ? = 44	89 – ? = 50	67 – ? = 62	55 – ? = 20
70 – ? = 68	100 – ? = 75	90 – ? = 82	10 – ? = 7
52 – ? = 32	25 – ? = 10	100 – ? = 25	36 – ? = 15
61 – ? = 31	100 – ? = 92	46 – ? = 44	74 – ? = 32
Kabang	Kaboom	Kabang	Kaboom

Figure 6.47 Challenge Cards

? – 10 = 55	__ – 15 = 22	55 – ? = 28	__ – 33 = 30
? – 70 = 80	__ – 20 = 50	81 – ? = 62	__ – 89 = 20
? – 50 = 34	__ – 35 = 75	100 – ? = 82	__ – 67 = 20
? – 47 = 40	__ – 90 = 10	40 – ? = 25	__ – 99 = 0
? – 39 = 61	__ – 8 = 92	52 – ? = 44	__ – 55 = 20
Kabang	Kaboom	Kabang	Kaboom

Section Summary

This is such a tricky concept for students. Although they are introduced to it in first grade, second and third graders still struggle with it. You have to spend a lot of time having students act it out and explain their thinking. Even when they are working with larger numbers and using the hundred grid as a scaffold, have them explain what they are doing and why. Of course, eventually you want students to be able to look at it and compute it mentally.

Overview

Figure 6.48 Overview

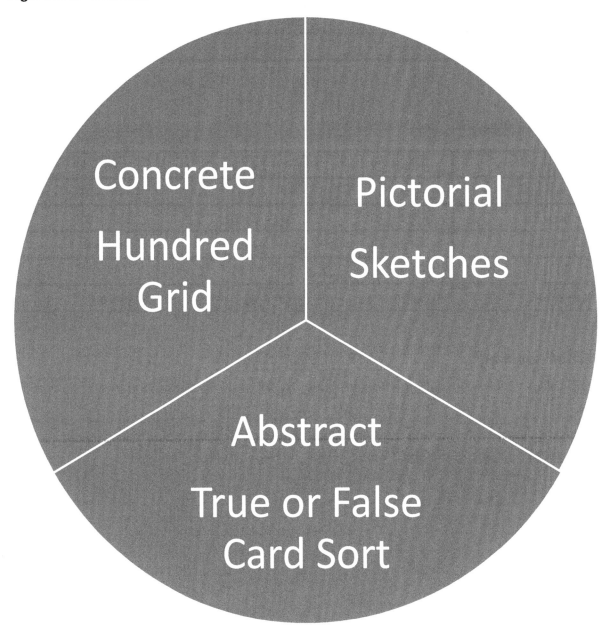

Figure 6.49 Planning Template

Equal Sign	
Big Idea: The equal sign means "the same as." **Enduring Understanding:** Students will understand that both sides of the equal sign should be the same amount. **Essential Question:** How do we determine if equations are true or false? **I can statement**: I can determine if equations are true or false.	**Materials** ♦ Tools: Cubes ♦ Templates: Ten Frame ♦ Cards ♦ Crayons
Vocabulary & Language Frames ♦ Group ♦ Addends ♦ Sum ♦ True ♦ False ♦ Same _____ is the same as _____. These are equal. These are not equal.	**Cycle of Engagement** **Concrete** **Pictorial** **Abstract** $50 - 40 = 10 + 0$

Figure 6.50 Differentiation

Three Differentiated Lessons

In this series of lessons, students are working on the concept of *the equal sign as meaning is the same as*. They are developing this concept through concrete activities, pictorial activities, and abstract activities. Everybody should do the cycle. Some students progress through it more quickly than others. Here are some things to think about as you do these lessons.

Emerging	On Grade Level	Above Grade Level
Students are introduced to this concept in first grade. Make sure they have a good handle on this with numbers within 20 before introducing larger numbers.	In second grade, extend the numbers. Students can model it and explain it. So do lots of this work where students are modeling it and explaining it with manipulatives, grids, and number lines.	Once they have the concept, play lots of abstract games, including card games, board games, and dice games.

 # Looking for Misunderstandings and Common Errors

It is important do many different explorations with the equal sign. You want students to be able to reason about numbers and not just give instant answers from what they visually see. They should always be asked to explain their thinking, defend their answer with numbers, words, and pictures and prove their thinking. Students have so much trouble with the equal sign. They often just think it means to put the answer. In this series of lessons, the focus is on students unpacking the equations to prove that they are equal or not equal.

Concrete Lesson

Figure 6.51 Concrete Introduction

	Introduction
Launch	**Teacher:** Today we are going to talk about the equal sign and how equations (number sentences) can be true or false.
	Vocabulary: addends, sum, true, false, same as
	Math Talk: _____ is the same as _____.
Model	I can prove my thinking with:

Counters

$6+2$ $=$ $5+3$

Number Path

1	2	3	4	5	6	7	8	9	10

Ten Frame

Picture

Teacher: Let's look at this problem. Is it true or false? How can I figure it out?
$20 + 30 = 30 + 20$
Tracie: We could use base ten blocks. So $50 = 50$, that's true.

Carlos: And it is the same numbers so it is the same.

Teacher: Tell me more about that.

Carlos: Well it's like a turn-around fact . . . if the numbers are the same on both sides, then it is the same.

Checking for Understanding	**Teacher:** What about $100 - 50 = 20 + 30$
	Tracie: That's true too because $100 - 50$ is 50 and $20 + 30$ is 50 too.
	Teacher: Who agrees? Why? Can you prove it another way?
	Mike: I can use a base ten sketch.
	$$\text{||| || TTTHL} \; = \; \text{|| |||}$$
	Teacher: Ok, so we all agree that one is true. Let's look at another one. Who wants to prove it? $23 + 2 = 21 + 4$
	Dan: I can prove it on my fingers. $23 + 2$ is 25 and $21 + 4$ is 25 so it's true.
	Kelly: I can prove it on my virtual rekenrek. It's true. It's the same amount.
	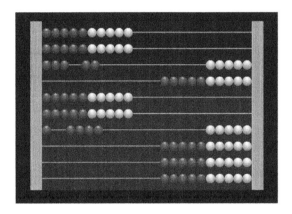
	Teacher: Ok, now I am going to give each of you some problems to sort into true and false. You will work with your partner.

Figure 6.52 Student Activity

	Student Activity
Guided Practice/ Checking for Understanding	Students go around the table and each of them model their equation and have to prove if it is true or false. They get to choose which tool they will use to justify their thinking. **Verna:** I have $\boxed{25 + 2 = 23 + 5}$ I counted on, using my fingers, and it is false. 27 is not the same as 28. **Todd:** I have $\boxed{24 + 23 = 70 + 5}$ I just thought like . . . 20 and 20 make 40 + 7 and that is not the same as 75.
Set Up for Independent Practice	**Teacher:** What did we do today? **Sean:** We were thinking about whether equations were true or false. We proved it with different tools. **Teacher:** Are all equations true? **Students:** No. **Tom:** Sometimes they are not true. **Teacher:** What was easy and what was tricky? **Claire:** Sometimes it is hard when you have big numbers. **Teacher:** What can you do then? **Tami:** You can use your counters or the rekenrek. **Teacher:** Yes, we can use our tools and our math strategies to think about it. Are there any questions or comments? Ok, you can now go to your workstation

Figure 6.53 Lesson Close

Close
◆ What did we do today? ◆ What was the math we were practicing? ◆ What are ways we were modeling our thinking? ◆ Was this easy or tricky? ◆ Turn to a partner and state one thing you learned today.

Pictorial Lesson

Figure 6.54 Pictorial Introduction

Introduction	
Launch	**Teacher:** Today we are going to talk about the equal sign and how equations (number sentences) can be true or false. **Vocabulary:** addends, sum, true, false, same as **Math Talk:** _____ is the same as _____.
Model	**Teacher:** Today we are going to continue working with the equal sign and finding out if an equation is true or false. (*Students should talk about what they did last time.*) **Teacher:** Today we are going to record our thinking with sketches. $$25 + 2 = 23 + 4$$ **Teacher:** How could we solve this problem with math sketches? **Lucy:** I know the answer, we can draw. It is true! **Teacher:** Who has a question? **Tom:** How do you know? **Lucy:** Because they both make 27.
Checking for Understanding	**Teacher:** Today we are going to get cards and model whether they are true or false by using math sketches.

Figure 6.55 Student Activity

	Student Activity
Guided Practice/ Checking for Understanding	**Kate:** I knew the answer because I just counted up and 17 + 2 is 19 and so is 19 − 0. I modeled it with the sketch. $$17 + 2 = 19 - 0$$ **How many did you draw?** **Did you get the same amount in both drawings?** **Is the equation true or false?**
Set Up for Independent Practice	*Students go around and everyone shows their work and shares their thinking.* **Teacher:** What math did we practice today? **Kate:** True and false equations. **Teacher:** What part is easy or tricky? **Tom:** Some of the numbers are easy to just count up. **Luke:** I think when it is two big numbers it can be tricky. **Teacher:** What do you have to do then? **Luke:** You can sketch and count. You could also add it up and compare. **Teacher:** Yes, you could do either of those. Really you could add it up and compare and then sketch to model it. Any more questions or comments? Ok, if not, go to your next station.

Figure 6.56 Lesson Close

Close
◆ What did we do today?
◆ What was the math we were practicing?
◆ Was this easy or tricky?
◆ Turn to a partner and state one thing you learned today.

Figure 6.57 Cards

True or False? $28 + 2 = 3 + 27$ How many did you draw on the left side? How many did you draw on the right side? Is it the same amount? Is this equation true or false?	**True or False?** $17 + 1 = 18 + 0$ How many did you draw on the left side? How many did you draw on the right side? Is it the same amount? Is this equation true or false?
True or False? $22 + 1 = 24 - 0$ How many did you draw on the left side? How many did you draw on the right side? Is it the same amount? Is this equation true or false?	**True or False?** $34 - 3 = 41 + 0$ How many did you draw on the left side? How many did you draw on the right side? Is it the same amount? Is this equation true or false?
True or False? $84 + 4 = 90 - 2$ How many did you draw on the left side? How many did you draw on the right side? Is it the same amount? Is this equation true or false?	**True or False?** $56 + 3 = 61 - 1$ How many did you draw on the left side? How many did you draw on the right side? Is it the same amount? Is this equation true or false?

Abstract Lesson

Figure 6.58 Abstract Introduction

Introduction	
Launch	**Teacher:** Today we are going to work on equations and sorting them. We have worked with tools to prove our thinking. We have worked with drawings. Now, we are going to focus on using our strategies to think about the equations. **Vocabulary:** addends, sum, true, false, same as **Math Talk:** _____ is the same as _____.
Model	Here is a true–false mat. You and your partner are going to get a baggie with equations. You are going to sort your problems on the mat between true and false. You have to think and talk with your partner about which ones are true and which ones are false. Can I just say, "Oh, I think this one is true . . . " without finding the number on both sides? **Taylor:** No. You have to find the number on both sides first and then you can say if it is true or false.
Checking for Understanding	**Teacher:** Who can explain the math we are working on? **Maite:** We are working on true and false sentences. Some sentences can be true and some can be false. *Students play the game with a partner. The teacher watches, comments, and asks questions.*

Figure 6.59 Student Activity

Student Activity	
Guided Practice/Checking for Understanding	**Teacher:** Ok Marissa, tell me why you said the statement you are holding is true. **Marissa:** 22 + 21 = 21 + 22 because it is a turn-around fact. If you turn them around, they are the same numbers. **Teacher:** Mike, tell me how you know your card is false. **Mike:** Because 34 + 21 = 21 + 5 isn't the same. 55 is not the same as 26.
Set Up for Independent Practice	*Students work with partners to sort the equations. The teacher asks questions to each partner pair. Then the teacher wraps up and dismisses students to workstations.*

Figure 6.60 Lesson Close

Close
♦ What did we do today? ♦ What was the math we were practicing? ♦ Was this easy or tricky? ♦ Turn to a partner and state one thing you learned today.

Figure 6.61 True/False Cards

$27 + 1 = 28 + 0$	$35 + 2 = 5 + 32$	$100 - 1 = 99 + 0$	$100 + 0 = 50 + 50$
$48 + 8 = 57 + 0$	$54 + 21 = 46 + 20$	$60 + 10 = 75 + 5$	$77 + 1 = 88 + 0$
$89 + 1 = 1 + 89$	$14 + 16 + 1 = 30 + 1$	$10 + 90 = 80 + 20$	$33 + 1 + 10 = 43 + 1$
$15 + 11 = 26 - 6$	$36 + 2 = 32 + 16$	$42 + 1 = 43 + 2$	$51 + 9 = 10 + 40$
$76 + 1 = 71 + 6$	$15 + 15 + 2 = 2 + 30$	$13 + 7 + 9 = 20 + 9$	$25 + 25 = 60 - 10$
$95 + 3 = 96 - 0$	$86 - 3 = 83 + 6$	$52 + 20 = 80 - 40$	$90 - 9 = 80 + 0$
$16 + 4 + 50 = 50 + 20$	$25 + 3 = 28 + 1$	$28 - 4 = 22 + 2$	$21 + 21 = 48 - 8$

Figure 6.62 True/False Mat

True	False

Section Summary

Working with the equal sign is always tricky. It has to be done with hands-on activities. Students need to actually build the facts so that they can see what the math is. They should absolutely act out the problems. By this I mean students getting up and act out 2 + 3 on one side of the equation and then 4 + 1 on the other side of the equation and they can then see that it is the same amount of kids on each side. Once they can see it, discuss and explain it, and then model it, draw it, and talk about the equal sign meaning *the same as*, then we know they are beginning to get it. After they can do it with the low numbers, expand the number range and use number lines and hundred grids. Spend all year working on exploring this concept through energizers, routines, and workstations.

Depth of Knowledge

Depth of Knowledge (Figure 6.63 & 6.64) is a framework that encourages us to ask questions that require students to think, reason, explain, defend, and justify their thinking (Webb, 2002). Here is snapshot of what that can look like in terms of place value work.

Figure 6.63 DOK Activities

	What are different strategies and models that we can use to teach missing numbers?	What are different strategies and models that we can use to teach arrays?	What are different strategies and models that we can use to model true or false statements?
DOK Level 1 (These are questions where students are required to simply recall/reproduce an answer/do a procedure.)	Solve ___ − 45 = 100	Draw an array that has 12 things in it.	Sort the equations into true and false piles.
DOK Level 2 (These are questions where students have to use information, think about concepts and reason.) This is considered a more challenging problem than a level 1 problem.	Discuss two different strategies for solving ___ − 45 = 100	Make an array of 12 things in three different ways. Explain why they are all true.	Pick two equations that are false. Explain why they are false and show how to make them true.
DOK Level 3 (These are questions where students have to reason, plan, explain, justify, and defend their thinking.)	Make your own missing number equation. Solve it. Explain and justify your thinking. ____ − ____ = ____	Pick a number and show different ways to make arrays with it. Explain your thinking.	Make five equations that are true and five equations that are false.

A great resource for asking open questions is Marion Small's *Good Questions: Great Ways to Differentiate Mathematics Instruction in the Standards-Based Classroom* (2017). Also, Robert Kaplinsky has done a great job in pushing our thinking forward with the Depth of Knowledge Matrices he created (https://robertkaplinsky.com/depth-knowledge-matrix-elementary-math/). Another

Figure 6.64 Asking rigorous questions

DOK 1	DOK 2 At this level, students explain their thinking.	DOK 3 At this level, students have to justify, defend, and prove their thinking with objects, drawings, and diagrams.
What is the answer to . . . ? Can you model the number? Can you model the problem? Is it true or false?	How do you know that the equation is correct? Can you pick the correct answer and explain why it is correct? How can you model that problem? What is another way to model that problem? Can you model that on the . . . ? Give me an example of a . . . type of problem . . . Which answer is incorrect? Explain your thinking.	Can you prove that your answer is correct? Prove that . . . Explain why that is the answer. . . . Show me how to solve that and explain what you are doing. Defend your thinking.

matrix example: http://images.pcmac.org/Uploads/ConecuhCountyBOE/ConecuhCountyBOE/Divisions/DocumentsCategories/Documents/Sample%20Mathematics.pdf (Kentucky Math Department, 2007)

Key Points

♦ Concrete, Pictorial, and Abstract
♦ Even and Odd Numbers
♦ Arrays
♦ Missing Numbers
♦ True/False Equations

Summary

When working on the big ideas of algebra in the primary grades, it is very important that students have a chance to reason about the situations and the numbers. Algebraic thinking must be developed from the beginning of school. In second grade, students are extending their ideas about the commutative and associative properties. These are fundamental building blocks to later algebraic work. Students must be given multiple opportunities to explore and discuss equations and their meanings with different types of manipulatives and drawings. They also are extending their work with the ideas of missing numbers and how to find them using various strategies.

In second grade, it is essential that students extend their thinking about equations and the meaning of the numbers and the equal sign. Students need opportunities to talk in small groups to discuss what is happening, to think about if they understand and agree with what is being said, and also to defend their own thinking and prove their ideas with manipulatives and drawings. In second grade, there are also a variety of new ideas, mainly even and odd numbers and arrays. So, as this work is being done in small groups, teachers should focus not only on the content but also on the practices. We are always integrating the mathematical practices/processes throughout our guided math lessons.

Reflection Questions

1. How are you currently teaching place value lessons?
2. Are you making sure that you do concrete, pictorial, and abstract activities?
3. What do your students struggle with the most, and what ideas are you taking away from this chapter that might inform your work around those struggles?

References

Blanton, M. L., & Kaput, J. J. (2003). Developing elementary teachers' "algebra eyes and ears". *Teaching Children Mathematics, 10*(2).

Blanton, M. L., Levi, L., Crites, T., Dougherty, B., & Zbiek, R. M. (2011). *Developing essential understanding of algebraic thinking for teaching mathematics in grades 3–5*. Series in Esential Understandings. Reston, VA: National Council of Teachers of Mathematics.

Blanton, M. L., Stroud, R. Stephens, A., Gardiner, A., Stylianou, D., Knuth, E., Isler-Baykal, & Strachota, S. (2019). Does early algebra matter? The effectiveness of an early algebra intervention in grades 3 to 5. *American Educational Research Journal* (Thousand Oaks, CA: Sage Publishing). https://doi.org/10.3102/0002831219832301

Carpenter, T., Levi, L., Franke, M., & Zeringue, J. (2005). Algebra in elementary school: Developing relational thinking. Zentralblatt für Didaktik der Mathematik, *37*, 53–59. https://doi.org/10.1007/BF02655897

Cristaldi, K. (1996). *Even Steven and odd Todd, level 3 (hello math reader)*. New York, NY: Scholastic.

Isler, I., Stephens, A., & Kang, H. (2016). Retrieved January 20, 2020, from www.nctm.org/Publications/Teaching-Children-Mathematics/Blog/Even-and-Odd-Numbers_-A-Journey-into-The-Algebraic-Thinking-Practice-of-Justification/

Kaput, J., Carraher, D., & Blanton, M. (2008). *Algebra in the early grades*. New York, NY: Routledge.

Kentucky Department of Education (2007). Support Materials for Core Content for Assessment Version 4.1 Mathematics. Retrieved from the internet on January 15th, 2017.

Math Their Way: Calendar Newsletter. Retrieved February 1, 2021 from https://www.center.edu/NEWSLETTER/newsletter.shtml

Small, M. (2017). *Good questions: Great ways to differentiate mathematics instruction in the standards-based classroom* (3rd ed.). New York, NY: Teachers College Press.

Tagle, J., Belecina, R., & Ocampo, J. (2016). *Developing algebraic thinking skills among grade three pupils through pictorial models*. Retrieved January 20, 2020, from www.researchgate.net/publication/320755828_Developing_Algebraic_Thinking_Skills_among_Grade_Three_Pupils_through_Pictorial_Models

Webb, N. (2002). *An analysis of the alignment between mathematics standards and assessments for three states*. Paper presented at the annual meeting of the American educational Research Association, New Orleans, LA.

7

Small-Group
Word Problem Lessons

It is important to teach about word problems in small guided math groups. Word problems are so full of potential, yet many students struggle with them! Researchers have found that story problems "are notoriously difficult to solve" (Cummins, Kintsh, Reusser, & Weimer, 1988). There are specific categories and levels of problems (Carpenter, Fennema, Franke, Levi, & Empson, 1999/2015; Fuchs et al., 2010; Jitendra, Hoff, & Beck, 1999). Students should get an opportunity to explore solving various problems in various ways. This work should be scaffolded in the guided math group.

Every state has outlined the types of problems by grades that students should be working on. In the guided math group, teachers scaffold the learning so that students are working in their zone of proximal development towards the grade-level standards. They range from easy to difficult. Also, even within categories, number ranges can vary and should be scaffolded.

We also look at several types of open problems, where students are much more responsible for actually making the problems. We discuss the 3-read protocol problems where students have to make the questions and then solve them. We look at numberless word problems that do what Bushart calls a "slow reveal," where the problem is slowly introduced to the students so that they can digest it in pieces (https://bstockus.wordpress.com/numberless-word-problems/). We also look at open problems, where there is context and then students make up the entire problem and solve it on a model (inspired by Marion Smalls, 2009).

Let's Talk About the Research!

- ◆ Students have a tendency to "suspend sense-making" when they are solving problems. They don't stop to reason through the problem (Schoenfeld, 1991; Verschaffel, Greer, & De Corte, 2000). We must find ways to slow the process down so they can think.
- ◆ Students develop a "compulsion to calculate" (Stacey & MacGregor, 1999) that can interfere with the development of the algebraic thinking that is needed to solve word problems (cited in www.cde.state.co.us/comath/word-problems-guide).
- ◆ Research consistently states that we should **never use key words**. From the beginning, teach students to reason about the context, not to depend on key words. See a great blog post that cites many articles on this: https://gfletchy.com/2015/01/12/teaching-key-words-forget-about-it/

In this chapter we will explore:

♦ Start Unknown Problems
♦ Part-Part Whole
♦ Compare
♦ Two-Step
♦ 3-Read Problems
♦ Picture Prompts
♦ Open Word Problems

Overview

Figure 7.1 Overview

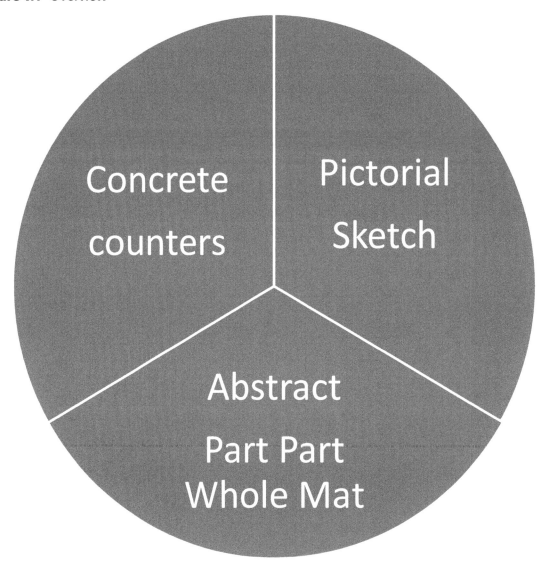

Figure 7.2 Planning Template

Start Unknown Word Problems

Big Idea: There are different types of word problems. In this type, we do not know the start.

Enduring Understanding: We can model problems in many ways.

Essential Question: What are the ways to model this type of problem?

I can statement: I can model addition word problems where the start is unknown.

Materials
- Tools: Cubes
- Templates: Ten Frame
- Cards
- Crayons

Cycle of Engagement

Concrete:

```
          10
  ┌──────────────┬──┬──┬──┐
  │      ?       │  │  │  │
  └──────────────┴──┴──┴──┘
```

Pictorial: Drawing

```
┌──┬──┬──┬──┬──┬──┬──┬──┬──┬──┐
│  │  │  │  │  │  │  │  │  │  │
├──┼──┼──┼──┼──┼──┼──┼──┼──┼──┤
│  │  │  │  │  │  │  │  │  │  │
├──┼──┼──┼──┼──┼──┼──┼──┼──┼──┤
│  │  │  │  │  │  │  │  │  │  │
└──┴──┴──┴──┴──┴──┴──┴──┴──┴──┘
```

Abstract: Match Addends and the Sum

Sue had some marbles. She got 3 more. Now she has 10. How many did she get?

Pick a model. Solve.
Number Path Grid Paper
Drawing Ten Frame

Vocabulary & Language Frames
- Count Up
- Count Back
- Addends
- Sum
- Difference

_____ had some_____.
_____ got ____more.
Now there are _____.
How many did they start with?

Figure 7.3 Differentiation

Three Differentiated Lessons		
In this series of lessons, students are working on the concept of *start unknown problems*. They are developing this concept through concrete activities, pictorial activities, and abstract activities. Everybody should do the cycle. Some students progress through it more quickly than others. Here are some things to think about as you do these lessons.		
Emerging	**On Grade Level**	**Above Grade Level**
Review adding. As you introduce this to students, do a lot of work by acting it out and then doing it with manipulatives. Be sure to have students draw what they acted out and connect it to number models.	The grade-level standard is that students can model it and explain it. So do lots of this work where students are modeling it and explaining it.	Extend the number range.

In many states, this is a second-grade problem. I find that the take from start unknown is actually easier than the add to start unknown, because at least in the former you can see all the parts. I tend to scaffold these in the beginning with 5, 10, and then 20 frames as visual scaffolds.

Figure 7.4 Anchor Chart

Solving Start Unknown Problems
Jane has some rings. She got 5 more. Now she has 7. How many did she have in the beginning?

Ten Frame:
$? + 5 = 7$

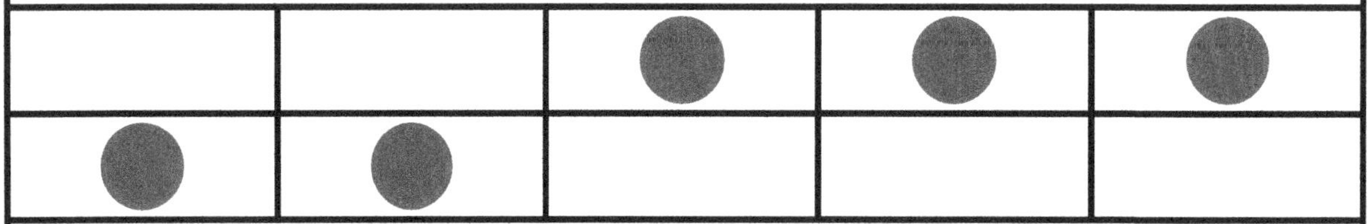

		●	●	●
●	●			

Insert

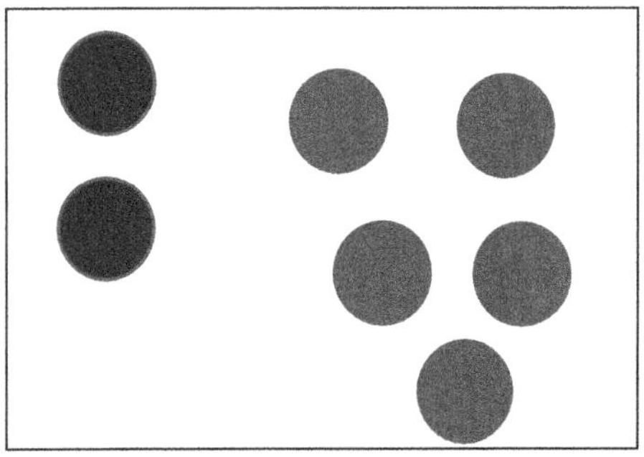

Concrete Lesson

Figure 7.5 Concrete Introduction

	Introduction
Launch	**Teacher:** Today we are going to work on solving word problems where the start is unknown. **Vocabulary:** add, start, word problem, count up **Math Talk:** I had some ____. I got ____ more. Now I have ____. How many did I have in the beginning?
Model	Listen to the problem. I had some jewels. I got 5 more. Now I have 10. How many did I have in the beginning? Now, who has some ideas how I could model that problem? **Jack:** You can count up. **Teacher:** Excellent! That is a strategy. Now, tell me how you could model that strategy? **Lucy:** We could use the counters. **Teacher:** Show me. **Lucy:** On the ten frame I have 5 and then to make 10 it would need 5 more. I put 5 to add up to 10. So I had 5 in the beginning. . .
	(ten frame: top row empty, bottom row five filled counters)
Checking for Understanding	**Teacher:** This is great! So we can model it with counters. What is another way to model that problem? **David:** I did it different. I put down 10 and then I took away 5. So I can see what I had.
	(ten frame: top row five filled counters, bottom row empty)
	Teacher: Ok. I am going to give each one of you your own problem. I want you to read it. Solve it. Be ready to share how you did it. I am going to watch you and if you need help, look at our anchor charts and of course you can ask me.

Figure 7.6 Student Activity

	Student Activity
Guided Practice/ Checking for Understanding	The teacher passes out the problems. Students pull a card and act out their problems. The students each get a chance to share their problem and explain how they solved it.
	Maria: My problem is this:
	Kim had some marbles. She got 3 more. Now, she has 6. How many did she have in the beginning?
	So, I used my ten frame and I put 6 down. I then took 3 off.
	Teacher: Why did you move 3 off?
	Maria: Because it said I got 3 more to make 6. So I took those 3 away to see what was in the beginning.
	Teacher: Who agrees with her?
	Hong: I do. I just know that 3 and 3 are 6.
	Teacher: That is great! You know it automatically. I also need you to show me how you might model it.
	Hong: I could count up on the number line. I could start at 3 and then jump to 6.
	Teacher: Does everybody see that? That even though we could know the answer because we know our facts, we still need to think about how to model our thinking. Our strategy might be counting up, or using doubles or something else, but our model shows our thinking.
Set Up for Independent Practice	*Every child shares out their problem and how they solved it.* **Teacher:** We are going to be talking more about this in the upcoming days. Are there any questions? What was interesting today? What was tricky?

Figure 7.7 Lesson Close

Close
◆ What did we do today?
◆ What was the math we were practicing?
◆ Was this easy or tricky?
◆ Turn to a partner and state one thing you learned today.

Figure 7.8 Start Unknown Problem Cards

The bakery had some pies. They made 5 more. Now they have 10. How many were there in the beginning? ___ + 5 = 10	There were some monkeys. 3 more came. Now there are 6. How many were there in the beginning? __ + 3 = 6
The bakery had some pies. They made 4 more. Now they have 7. How many did they make? ___ + 4 = 7	There were some monkeys. 10 more came. Now there are 18. How many were there in the beginning? ____ + 10 = 18
The bakery had some pies. They made 8 more. Now they have 12. How many did they have in the beginning? ___ + 8 = 12	There were some monkeys. 5 more came. Now there are 15. How many were there in the beginning? ____ + 5 = 15
The bakery had some pies. They made 7 more. Now they have 14. How many did they have in the beginning? ___ + 7 = 14	There were some monkeys. 10 more came. Now there are 20. How many where there in the beginning? ___ + 10 = 20
The bakery had pies. They made 4. Now they have 10. How many did they have in the beginning? ____ + 4 = 10	There was some monkeys. 12 more came. Now there are 15. How many were there in the beginning? ___ + 12 = 15

For the challenge level, have the students use base ten blocks for manipulatives.

Figure 7.9 Challenge Level Cards

The bakery had some pies. They made 25 more. Now they have 30. How many were there in the beginning? ___+ 25 = 30	There were some monkeys. 30 more came. Now there are 60. How many were there in the beginning? ___ + 30 = 60
The bakery had some pies. They made 14 more. Now they have 20. How many did they make? ___ + 14 = 20	There were some monkeys. 40 more came. Now there are 58. How many were there in the beginning? ____ + 40 = 58
The bakery had some pies. They made 18 more. Now they have 20. How many did they have in the beginning? ___ + 18 = 20	There were some monkeys. 50 more came. Now there are 100. How many were there in the beginning? ____ + 50 = 100
The bakery had some pies. They made 70 more. Now they have 84. How many did they have in the beginning? ___ + 70 = 84	There were some monkeys. 20 more came. Now there are 50. How many where there in the beginning? ___ + 20 = 50
The bakery had some pies. They made 4. Now they have 10. How many did they have in the beginning? ____ + 4 = 10	There was some monkeys. 12 more came. Now there are 15. How many were there in the beginning? ___ + 12 = 15

Pictorial Lesson

Figure 7.10 Pictorial Introduction

	Introduction
Launch	**Teacher:** Today we are going to work on solving word problems where the start is unknown. **Vocabulary:** add, start, word problem, count up, number sentence (equation), missing number **Math Talk:** There were ____. _____ more came. Now there are ___. How many were there in the beginning?
Model	**Teacher:** There were some monkeys. 10 more came. Now there are 12. How many were there in the beginning? **Teacher:** Does everybody see this model. Who can explain it? **Ted:** You drew 12 because that is the total. You took away the 10 that came. That shows how many were in the beginning. **Teacher:** So, do you see how that works? Who wants to try one?
Checking for Understanding	**Marta:** I want to try one. > The bakery had some cupcakes. They made 5 more. Now there are 10. How many did they make? **Marta:** I drew 10 because that is what there is now. I took away the 5 so I can see that there were 5 before to make 10.

Figure 7.11 Student Activity

	Student Activity
Guided Practice/ Checking for Understanding	The teacher passes out word problem cards. Students pull a card and model their problems. The students each get a chance to share their problem and explain how they solved it.
	Maria: My problem is this:
	Hong had some marbles. He got 4 more. Now he has 7. How many did he have in the beginning?
	Set-up Equation
	$$m + 4 = 7$$
	Sketch
	∘∘ ◌ ◌ ◌ ◌ ◌
	Equation
	$$3 + 4 = 7$$
	Maria: I drew 7 and then I took away 4 so I had 3 in the beginning because 3 and 4 make 7.
	Teacher: So what was your strategy?
	Maria: I know that 4 and 3 make 7. I drew the circles for the model.
	Teacher: Who agrees with her?
	Grace: I do.
	David: I counted up on my fingers.
Set up for Independent Practice	**Teacher:** That is great! You know it automatically. Remember even if you just know it, you should be able to model it and explain it.
	Teacher: Does everybody see that? That even though we could know the answer because we know our facts, we still need to think about how to model our thinking. Our strategy might be, counting up, or using doubles or something else, but our model shows our thinking.
	The teacher gives everybody a chance to do and discuss a problem. After everyone has shared, the lesson ends.
	We are going to be talking more about this in the upcoming days. Are there any questions? What was interesting today? What was tricky?

Figure 7.12 Cards

Hong had some marbles. He got 9 more. Now he has 15. How many did he have in the beginning? Set-up Equation Sketch Equation	Grace had some marbles. He got 9 more. Now he has 20. How many did he have in the beginning? Set-up Equation Sketch Equation
Jamal had some toy trucks. He got 25 more. Now he has 45. How many did he have in the beginning? Set-up Equation Sketch Equation	Jamal had some toy cars. He got 50 more. Now he has 70. How many did he have in the beginning? Set-up Equation Sketch Equation
Kiyana had some rings. She got 20 more. Now she has 25. How many did she have in the beginning? Set-up Equation Sketch Equation	Maria had some bracelets. She got 20 more. Now she has 40. How many did she have in the beginning? Set-up Equation Sketch Equation
David had some toy cars. He got 8 more. Now he has 20. How many did he have in the beginning? Set-up Equation Sketch Equation	Kelly had some marbles. She got 50 more. Now she has 100. How many did she have in the beginning? Set-up Equation Sketch Equation

Figure 7.13 Lesson Close

Close

- What did we do today?
- What was the math we were practicing?
- Was this easy or tricky?
- Turn to a partner and state one thing you learned today.

Abstract Lesson

Figure 7.14 Abstract Introduction

<table>
<tr><th colspan="2">Introduction</th></tr>
<tr>
<td>Launch</td>
<td>

Teacher: Today we are going to work on solving word problems where the start is unknown.

Vocabulary: add, start unknown, word problem, count up, number sentence (equation)

Math Talk: There were some _____. ___ more came. Now there are ____. How many were there in the beginning?

Teacher: Everybody get your part-part whole mats ready. I am going to read the problem and then you will illustrate it and show it to the group. We will take turns explaining our thinking. Here we go.

</td>
</tr>
<tr>
<td>Model</td>
<td>

Teacher: You all fill in your part-part whole mats.

18	
?	10

Luke had some marbles. He got 10 more. Now he has 18. How many did he have in the beginning?

</td>
</tr>
<tr>
<td>Checking for Understanding</td>
<td>

Teacher: Does everybody see this model. Who can explain it?

Ted: The 18 on top is the total. The 10 is what he got. The question mark is the missing number. It's what we had in the beginning.

Teacher: How do we find the missing number?

Connie: We could think 10 plus what makes 18.

Teacher: Yes, we could do that. Everybody get their part-part whole mats ready. I am going to read the problem and then you will illustrate it and show it to the group. We will take turns explaining our thinking. Here we go.

</td>
</tr>
</table>

Figure 7.15 Student Activity

	## Student Activity
Guided Practice/ Checking for Understanding	The teacher reads different problems. The children solve the problems on their part-part whole mats and show them to the group. Each time, a different student explains how they solved the problem. **Teacher:** There were some monkeys. 30 more came. Now there a 40. How many came? | 40	
?	30 | **Josephine explains:** I put 40 at the top because that is the total. I put 30 because that is how many came. I put the question mark at the beginning. **Timmy:** The answer is 10 because 10 and 30 make 40. **Teacher:** Yes. *Everybody models the problems and shows it on their part-part whole mast. Some students have the numbers in the wrong place and they erase and fix it. The teacher reminds everybody that it is ok to make mistakes because that means you are trying and when you keep trying you will get it.* **Teacher:** We are going to be talking more about this in the upcoming days. Are there any questions? What was interesting today? What was tricky? **Kelly:** I think it is tricky to know where the numbers go. **Teacher:** Yes, it can be tricky. Who can give us some ideas on how to work with the numbers? **Jamal:** You have to look at the total and that goes at the top. The other number is how many there were so that goes in this box. The missing number always goes here. **Teacher:** Does it always go there or does it depend on the type of problem? **Jamal:** It depends on the type of problem. But in these, it always goes here. **Teacher:** What do you mean in these types of problems? **Carol:** Well we know the change and we know the end. See, here is what we are looking for, so the question mark goes here.
Set up for Independent Practice	**Teacher:** Ok then. Anymore comments or questions. If not, you all can go to your next station as soon as I ring the rotation bell.

Figure 7.16 Lesson Close

Close
◆ What did we do today?
◆ What was the math we were practicing?
◆ Was this easy or tricky?
◆ Turn to a partner and state one thing you learned today.

Figure 7.17 Problem Solving Cards

Hong had some marbles. He got 10 more. Now he has 20. How many did he have in the beginning?	Grace had some marbles. He got 15 more. Now he has 30. How many did he have in the beginning?
Jamal had some toy trucks. He got 20 more. Now he has 40. How many did he have in the beginning?	Jamal had some toy cars. He got 50 more. Now he has 100. How many did he have in the beginning?
Kiyana had some rings. She got 10 more. Now she has 25. How many did she have in the beginning?	Maria had some bracelets. She got 20 more. Now she has 30. How many did she have in the beginning?
David had some toy cars. He got 11 more. Now he has 20. How many did he have in the beginning?	Kelly had some marbles. She got 60 more. Now she has 100. How many did she have in the beginning?

Section Summary

Start unknown problems can be very tricky. The add to start unknown problems should be scaffolded with counters and in part-part whole mats. The counters provide that physical contact so students can move them around to make sense of the problem. The part-part whole mat is a great abstract visual because students can see the numbers. Number lines and number grids are also great abstract visual scaffolds because students can see the numbers. Eventually you want students to be able to reason it out with just equations and/or mental math.

Overview

Figure 7.18 Overview

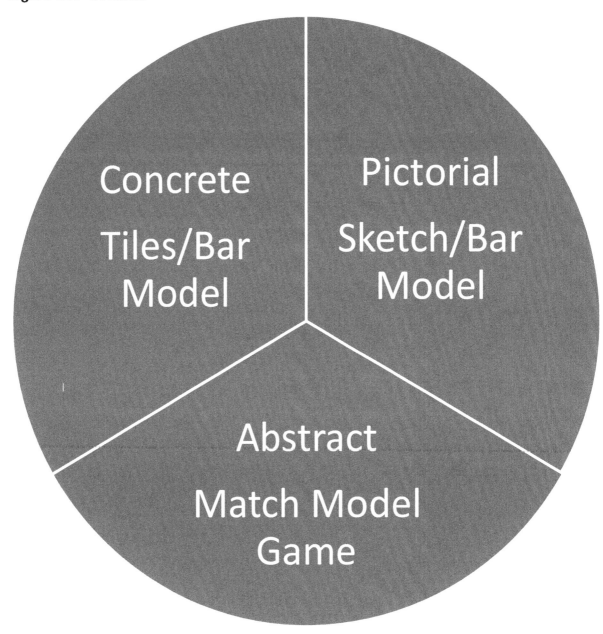

Figure 7.19 Planning Template

Part-Part Whole Problems

Big Idea: There are different types of word problems. In this type, we know one part but we don't know the other. We do know the total though.

Enduring Understanding: We can model problems in many ways.

Essential Question: What are the ways to model this type of problem?

I can statement: I can model part-part whole word problems.

Materials

♦ Tools: Cubes
♦ Templates: Ten Frame
♦ Cards
♦ Crayons

Cycle of Engagement

Concrete:

Whole	
Part	Part

Pictorial: Drawing

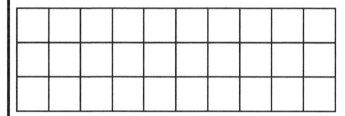

Abstract: Match Addends and the Sum

Sue had 17 marbles. Ten of them were big and the rest were small. How many were small?

17 − 10 = ?
10 + ? = 17

Vocabulary & Language Frames

♦ Count Up
♦ Count Back
♦ Addends
♦ Sum
♦ Difference

___ and ___ make ___.

Figure 7.20 Differentiated Lessons

Three Differentiated Lessons

In this series of lessons, students are working on the concept of *part-part whole problems*. They are developing this concept through concrete activities, pictorial activities, and abstract activities. Everybody should do the cycle. Some students progress through it more quickly than others. Here are some things to think about as you do these lessons.

Emerging	On Grade Level	Above Grade Level
Review adding. As you introduce this to students, do a lot of work by acting it out and then doing it with manipulatives. Be sure to have students draw what they acted out and connect it to number models.	The grade-level standard is that students can model it and explain it. So do lots of this work where students are modeling it and explaining it.	Extend the number range.

There are three types of part-part whole problems. Students have difficulty with the part-part whole with part unknown problems. Also, the both addends unknown problems are tricky for most of the students.

Figure 7.21 Anchor Chart

Solving Part-Part Whole Problems With Tape Diagrams

Jane has 7 rings. Five rings are square and the rest are circles. How many are circles?

1 Inch Tiles:

$5 + ? = 7$

7

Bar Diagram

5 square	? circles

Concrete Lesson

Figure 7.22 Concrete Introduction

Introduction	
Launch	**Teacher:** Today we are going to work on word problems. We are word problem detectives. We are going to be looking and thinking about the parts we know and don't know! **Vocabulary:** part- part whole, whole, word problem, count up, **Math Talk:** The whole is _____. One part is _____. The other part is _____.
Model	**Teacher:** Listen to the problem: Jamal had 7 marbles. 6 were big and the rest were small. How many small ones does he have? **Lucy:** 1 because 6 + 1 is 7. **Teacher:** Let's model it with our tiles first. **Jack:** We need 1 more. Because 6 plus 1 is 7. Here is the model. **Teacher:** So what do we see? **David:** We see the 6 and we can count 6–7. We need 1 more.
Checking for Understanding	**Teacher:** Well, he has 7 marbles in all. What are we looking for? **Tara:** We want to know how many small marbles he has. **Teacher:** Can you draw that as a bar model? Remember how we were talking in whole group about how the different colors can each be a rectangle? **Keith:** Yes. *Teacher reads 2 more problems that the group discusses.* **Teacher:** Ok. I am going to give each one of you your own problem. I want you to read it. Solve it. Be ready to share how you did it. I am going to watch you and if you need help, look at our anchor charts and of course you can ask me.

Figure 7.23 Concrete Activity

	Concrete Student Activity
Guided Practice/ Checking for Understanding	The teacher passes out the problems. Students pull a card and act out their problems. The students each get a chance to share their problem and explain how they solved it. **Timmy:** My problem is this: There were 10 marbles. 8 were orange. The rest were yellow. **Kelly:** So, first I built the 8 and then added 2 more tiles. And then I drew the big rectangle and made it 8 and the small rectangle and made it the 2. I put the 10 on top. 10 8 2 **Teacher:** Are you sure that is the way to do it? **Kelly:** Yes. I know that 8 plus 2 is 10. The tape diagram looks like this. **Teacher:** That is great! Who wants to go next. **Hong:** My problem said, "Jane had 8 marbles. 4 were red and the rest were yellow. How many were yellow?" That's easy because 4 and 4 make 8. **Teacher:** Can you model it with the tiles and make a tape diagram? **Hong:** Yes!
Set up for Independent Practice	*Every child shares out their problem and how they solved it.* **Teacher:** We are going to be talking more about this in the upcoming days. Are there any questions? What was interesting today? What was tricky?

Figure 7.24 Lesson Close

Close
◆ What did we do today? ◆ What was the math we were practicing? ◆ Was this easy or tricky? ◆ Turn to a partner and state one thing you learned today.

Figure 7.25 Part-Part Whole Cards

There are 6 counters. 3 are red and the rest are yellow. How many are yellow?	There are 15 counters. 5 are red and the rest are yellow. How many are yellow?
There are 14 counters. 2 are red and the rest are yellow. How many are yellow?	There are 3 counters. 1 is red and the rest are yellow. How many are yellow?
There are 18 counters. 6 are red and the rest are yellow. How many are yellow?	There are 8 counters. 4 are red and the rest are yellow. How many are yellow?
There are 19 counters. 7 are red and the rest are yellow. How many are yellow?	There are 14 counters. 11 are red and the rest are yellow. How many are yellow?
There are 12 counters. 10 are red and the rest are yellow. How many are yellow?	There are 10 counters. 9 are red and the rest are yellow. How many are yellow?
There are 8 counters. 2 are red and the rest are yellow. How many are yellow?	There are 8 counters. 5 are red and the rest are yellow. How many are yellow?
There are 2 counters. 1 is red and the rest are yellow. How many are yellow?	There are 10 counters. 7 are red and the rest are yellow. How many are yellow?

Pictorial Lesson

Figure 7.26 Pictorial Introduction

	Introduction
Launch	**Teacher:** Today we are going to continue to work on solving word problems and modeling them with a tape diagram. **Vocabulary:** part-part whole, word problem, count up, number sentence (equation), missing number **Math Talk:** The whole is _____. One part is _____. The other part is _____.
Model	**Teacher:** There were 18 animals. 5 were elephants and the rest were monkeys. How many monkeys were there? How could we model this problem with a tape diagram? **Don:** We have a part-part whole mat. The 18 goes at the top and we put the 5 elephants on one side and the question mark on the other. 18 <table><tr><td>5 elephants</td><td>? monkeys</td></tr></table> **Teacher:** Does everybody see this model? Who can explain it? Are the numbers in the right place? **Grace:** Yes. We have 18 total. 5 plus something makes 18. **Teacher:** How can we figure out the answer? **Tom:** You can take 18 and count back 5. . . so 18 – 17, 16, 15, 14, 13 and you get 13. So the answer is 13.
Checking for Understanding	**Marta:** I want to try one. > The bakery had 12 cupcakes. 6 were strawberry, the rest were vanilla. How many were vanilla? **Marta:** So I know the answer is 6 because 6 and 6 make 12. So there are 2 rectangles but they are the same size. *This conversation continues with the students using tape diagrams to model their stories.*

Figure 7.27 Student Activity

	Student Activity
Guided Practice/ Checking for Understanding	The teacher passes out word problem cards. Students pull a card and model their problems. The students each get a chance to share their problem and explain how they solved it. **Maria: My problem is this:** There were 19 pies. 10 were lemon and the rest were apple. How many were apple? **Maria:** I know that 10 and 9 make 19. Here is my model. <div align="center">19 pies</div>
		10 lemon	9 apple
Set Up for Independent Practice	**Teacher:** Does everybody see that? You all are doing really well modeling with the tape diagram. *The teacher gives everybody a chance to do and discuss a problem. After everyone has shared, the lesson ends.* **Teacher:** We are going to be talking more about this in the upcoming days. Are there any questions? What was interesting today? What was tricky?

Figure 7.28 Lesson Close

Close
♦ What did we do today?   ♦ What was the math we were practicing?   ♦ Was this easy or tricky?   ♦ Turn to a partner and state one thing you learned today.

Figure 7.29 Tape Diagram Cards

There were 10 butterflies. 7 were red and the rest were orange. How many were orange? Model with the tape diagram.	There were 15 butterflies. 10 were green and the rest were orange. How many were orange? Model with the tape diagram.
There were 60 butterflies. 20 were yellow and the rest were orange. How many were orange? Model with the tape diagram.	There were 10 butterflies. 5 were red and the rest were orange. How many were orange? Model with the tape diagram.
There were 10 kids. 3 were boys and the rest were girls. How many were girls?	The bakery made 50 cookies. 40 were chocolate chip and the rest were oatmeal. How many were oatmeal?
The bakery made 50 cupcakes. 25 were chocolate chip and the rest were oatmeal. How many were oatmeal?	The bakery made 100 pies. 85 were apple, 10 were lemon, and the rest were pumpkin. How many were pumpkin?
The fruit stand had 20 bags of fruit. 14 were strawberries and the rest were cherries. How many were cherries?	The fruit stand had 20 bags of fruit. 8 were strawberries, 4 were bananas, and the rest were cherries. How many were cherries?
The bakery made 50 cupcakes. 15 were chocolate chip and the rest were oatmeal. How many were oatmeal?	The bakery made 100 pies. 20 were apple, 30 were lemon, and the rest were pumpkin. How many were pumpkin?
The fruit stand had 20 bags of fruit. 10 were strawberries and the rest were cherries. How many were cherries?	The fruit stand had 20 bags of fruit. 10 were strawberries, 5 were bananas, and the rest were cherries. How many were cherries?

There were 10 butterflies. 7 were red and the rest were orange. How many were orange? Model with the tape diagram. ┌──────────────────────┐ │ │ └──────────────────────┘	There were 15 butterflies. 10 were green and the rest were orange. How many were orange? Model with the tape diagram. ┌──────────────────────┐ │ │ └──────────────────────┘
The bakery made 100 cupcakes. 50 were chocolate chip and the rest were oatmeal. How many were oatmeal? ┌──────────────────────┐ │ │ └──────────────────────┘	The bakery made 100 pies. 70 were apple, 30 were lemon, and the rest were pumpkin. How many were pumpkin? ┌──────────────────────┐ │ │ └──────────────────────┘
The fruit stand had 45 bags of fruit. 15 were strawberries and the rest were cherries. How many were cherries? ┌──────────────────────┐ │ │ └──────────────────────┘	The fruit stand had 35 bags of fruit. 10 were strawberries, 5 were bananas, and the rest were cherries. How many were cherries? ┌──────────────────────┐ │ │ └──────────────────────┘

Abstract Lesson

Figure 7.30 Abstract Introduction

Introduction

Launch	**Teacher:** Today we are going to work on solving word problems where we don't know one of the parts. We are working on tape diagrams. Vocabulary: part-part whole, whole, part, word problem, count up, number sentence (equation) **Math Talk:** The whole is _____. One part is _____. The other part is _____. **Teacher:** Today we are going to play a match game. We have to find the word problem, the part-part whole diagram and the number sentence that all match. There are three problems that are all mixed up in the bags. I am going to let you work with your partner to talk and discuss the problems and match them up. I am going to listen and ask you questions. Let's do one together.
	<table><tr><td colspan="2">7</td></tr><tr><td>5</td><td>?</td></tr></table> 5 + 2 = 7 Luke had 7 marbles. 5 were red and the rest were yellow. How many were yellow?
Model	**Teacher:** Does everybody see this model. Who can explain it? **Ted:** The 7 on top is the total. The 5 are the red ones. The question mark are the yellow ones. **Teacher:** How do we find the missing number? **Connie:** We could count up to 7 from 5.
Checking for Understanding	**Teacher:** Yes, we could do that. Are you all ready to work with your partner on your problems? Ok go!

Figure 7.31 Student Activity

	Student Activity
Guided Practice/ Checking for Understanding	The teacher watches the students as they work together to discuss and match the problems. **Teacher watches Leah and Tom:** How do you know this equation goes with the problem? **Leah:** Because it says 10 + what number and in the problem we know there are 17 and we are looking for the 10 plus what number.
	  Luke had 17 marbles. 10 were red and the rest were yellow. How many were yellow?
Set up for Independent Practice	The teacher continues to watch the groups as they work on matching their problems. When everyone has finished, the teacher asks the students to explain their thinking. She also asks them what was easy and what was tricky.

Figure 7.32 Lesson Close

Close
♦ What did we do today? ♦ What was the math we were practicing? ♦ Was this easy or tricky? ♦ Turn to a partner and state one thing you learned today.

Figure 7.33 Word problem cards

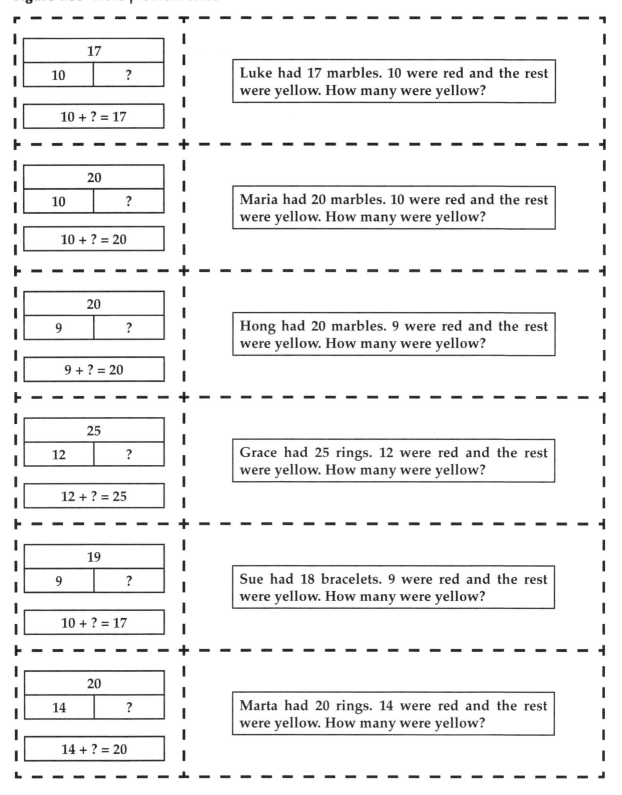

40	
20	?

20 + ? = 40

Kelly had 40 marbles. 20 were red and the rest were yellow. How many were yellow?

50	
12	?

12 + ? = 50

Mike had 50 toy trucks. 12 were red and the rest were yellow. How many were yellow?

Section Summary

In this section, we talked about solving part-part whole problems with different models. In second grade, it is important that students learn how to use tape diagrams to model their thinking. So we have shown how students can use 1-inch tiles as the scaffold for doing this concretely and then drawing out what they did. They could also use Cuisenaire™ rods to do this. The next step is to have the rectangle and have the students think about how to partition it to show the different parts. We also showed a way to get students to practice modeling in the part-part whole diagram and with an equation with a symbol for the unknown.

Overview

Figure 7.34 Overview

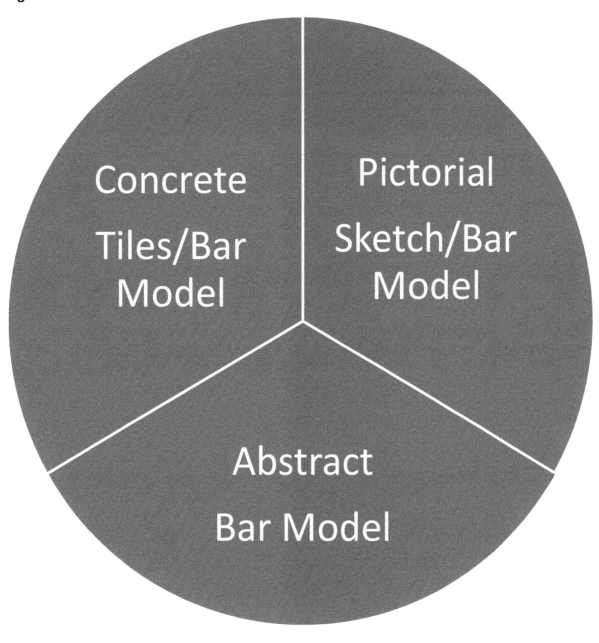

Figure 7.35 Planning Template

Two-Step Word Problems

Big Idea: There are different types of word problems. In this type, we are working on word problems that have two parts. **Enduring Understanding:** We can model problems in many ways. **Essential Question:** What are the ways to model this type of problem? **I can statement:** I can model word problems with two parts.	**Materials** ♦ Tools: Cubes ♦ Templates: Ten Frame ♦ Cards ♦ Crayons
Cycle of Engagement **Concrete:** Marta had 4 marbles. Todd had 1 more than she had. How many did they have altogether? 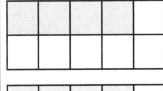 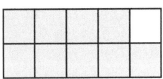 **Pictorial:** Drawing **Abstract:** Mental Math $4 + 4 + 1 = 9$	**Vocabulary & Language Frames** ♦ Count Up ♦ Count Back ♦ Addends ♦ Difference _____ take away ____ is _____.

Figure 7.36 Differentiation

Three Differentiated Lessons		
In this series of lessons, students are working on the concept of *two-step problems*. They are developing this concept through concrete activities, pictorial activities, and abstract activities. Everybody should do the cycle. Some students progress through it more quickly than others. Here are some things to think about as you do these lessons.		
Emerging Level	**On Grade Level**	**Above Grade Level**
Review adding and subtracting. As you introduce this to students, do a lot of work by acting it out and then doing it with manipulatives. Be sure to have students draw what they acted out and connect it to number models. They should have a good command of single-step problems.	Students start working on two-step problems in second grade. It is important that they have a good grasp of single-step problems before they start doing deep independent dives on two-step problems.	Extend the number range.

In many states, this is a second-grade problem. There are five types of two-step problems. The first type is same operation, two steps. The second type is addition and subtraction. The third, fourth, and fifth levels just mix problem types. Focus on using manipulatives and drawings and then relating that to the equations.

Figure 7.37 Anchor Chart

Solving Two-Step Problems

Jane has 5 rings. Her sister has 2 more than she does. How many do they have altogether?

Ten Frame:

Jane: 5

Sister: 5 + 2

5 + 7 = 12

Part 1: What do we know?
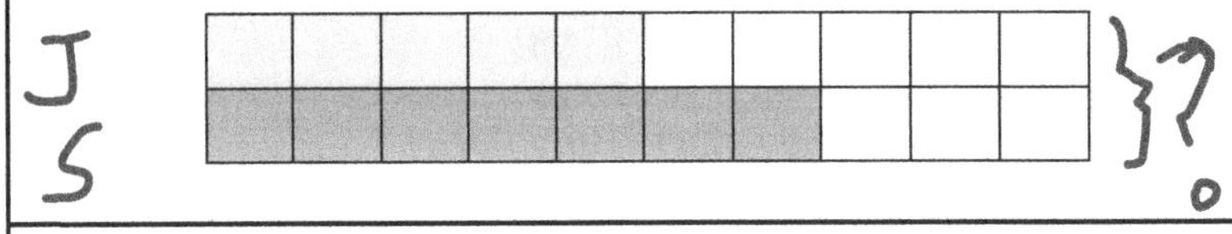 J 5 }? o
Sketch }12

Concrete Lesson

Figure 7.38 Concrete Introduction

	Introduction
Launch	**Teacher:** Today we are going to work on two-step problems. **Vocabulary:** compare, addends, sum, altogether **Math Talk:** ___ has ___. ___has ___ more. How many do they have altogether?
Model	The teacher gives students a mat to scaffold thinking. **Teacher:** Let's build it first with cubes and then color it. <table><tr><td>**Part 1: What do we know?**</td></tr><tr><td>(blank ten-frame grid)</td></tr><tr><td>**Part 2: What's next?** Solution:</td></tr></table> **Teacher:** Listen to this problem. John had 7 marbles. Tim had 1 more than he had. How many did they have altogether? **Katie:** I built it and then I colored it. We have to color John's marbles and then Tim's. Then we have to add them together. I got 15. <table><tr><td>**Part 1: What do we know?**</td></tr><tr><td>(colored cube rows J and T with }?)</td></tr><tr><td>**Part 2: What's next?** 7 + 8 = 15 Solution: 15</td></tr></table>

Checking for Understanding	**Teacher:** Ok. Does everybody see what Katie did? Does it make sense?
	Here's another problem:
	Michael had 8 marbles. Joe had 2 less than he did. How many do they have altogether?
	Teacher: Ok. Who can explain a way to do it?
	Timothy: I built 8 on top and 6 on the bottom. Then I colored Michael's marbles and then Joe's. Then we add them together.
	Teacher: Who agrees and why?
	Yessenia: I agree. I got 14 too.
	The teacher reads two more problems that the group discusses.
	Teacher: Ok. I am going to give each one of you your own problem. I want you to read it. Solve it. Be ready to share how you did it. I am going to watch you and if you need help, look at our anchor charts and of course you can ask me.

Figure 7.39 Student Activity

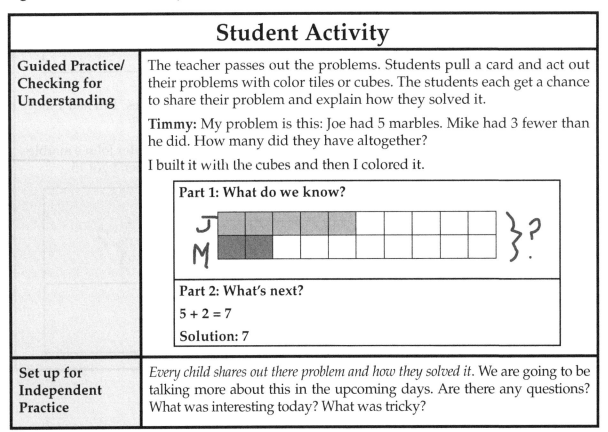

Student Activity

Guided Practice/ Checking for Understanding	The teacher passes out the problems. Students pull a card and act out their problems with color tiles or cubes. The students each get a chance to share their problem and explain how they solved it.
	Timmy: My problem is this: Joe had 5 marbles. Mike had 3 fewer than he did. How many did they have altogether?
	I built it with the cubes and then I colored it.
	Part 1: What do we know? **Part 2: What's next?** 5 + 2 = 7 Solution: 7
Set up for Independent Practice	*Every child shares out there problem and how they solved it.* We are going to be talking more about this in the upcoming days. Are there any questions? What was interesting today? What was tricky?

Figure 7.40 Lesson Close

Close
♦ What did we do today?
♦ What was the math we were practicing?
♦ Was this easy or tricky?
♦ Turn to a partner and state one thing you learned today.

Figure 7.41 Word Problem Cards.

Part 1: What do we know?
Part 2: What's next?
Solution:
Part 1: What do we know?
Part 2: What's next?
Solution:

Figure 7.42 Two-Step Word Problems

Kelly had 5 rings. Sue had 3 more than she had. How many did they have altogether?	Sue had 9 marbles. Joe had 1 less than she did. How many did they have altogether?
Marta had 5 rings. Lucy had 3 more than she had. How many did they have altogether?	Luisa had 9 marbles. Janet had 1 less than she did. How many did they have altogether?
Kiyana had 9 rings. Sue had 2 fewer than she did. How many did they have altogether?	Sue had 9 marbles. Joe had 1 more than she had. How many did they have altogether?

Pictorial Lesson

Figure 7.43 Pictorial Introduction

	Introduction
Launch	**Teacher:** Today we are going to work more on our 2-part problems. **Vocabulary:** take away, subtract, add, addend, sum, altogether **Math Talk:** Lara had ___ marbles. Her brother had ____ more. How many did they have altogether?
Model	**Teacher:** We are going to model it on the mats today. We are not going to build it with the cubes this time. *Sharon had 3 marbles. Jake had 5 more than she did. How many did they have altogether?* **Tom:** That's easy. I colored her 3 and then his 5 more and then I added them altogether. <table><tr><td>**Part 1: What do we know?**</td></tr><tr><td>**Part 2: What's next?** 3 + 8 = 11 Solution: 11</td></tr></table>
Checking for Understanding	**Teacher:** Excellent work. How do you know you are correct? **Tom:** I could double-check it. I can make sure I colored the right amounts. I check the adding.

Figure 7.44 Student Activity

	Student Activity
Launch	The teacher passes out word problem cards. Students pull a card and tell their problems. The students each get a chance to share their problem and explain how they solved it. This time they don't build it first. They model it with grid paper only. **Maria:** My problem is this: *There were 7 monkeys. There were 3 more elephants than monkeys. How many animals were there altogether?* **Part 2: What's next?** 7 + 10 = 17 Solution: 17
Set up for Independent Practice	*Teacher gives everybody a chance to do and discuss a problem. After everyone has shared the lesson ends.* **Teacher:** We are going to be talking more about this in the upcoming days. Are there any questions? What was interesting today? What was tricky?

Figure 7.45 Two-Step Word Problem Cards

Larry had 5 marbles. Mike had 2 more than he had. How many did they have altogether?

Part 1: What do we know?

Part 2: What's next?

Equation:

Solution:

Noelle had 8 marbles. Mike had 2 more than she had. How many did they have altogether?

Part 1: What do we know?

Part 2: What's next?

Equation:

Solution:

Kristi had 10 marbles. Mike had 2 fewer than she did. How many did they have altogether?

Part 1: What do we know?

Part 2: What's next?

Equation:

Solution:

Marcus had 7 marbles. Luke had 5 fewer than he did. How many did they have altogether?

Part 1: What do we know?

Part 2: What's next?

Equation:

Solution:

Lucia had 8 marbles. Marta had 9. How many did they have altogether?

Part 1: What do we know?

Part 2: What's next?

Equation:

Solution:

Cathy had 9 marbles. Marta had 10. How many did they have altogether?

Part 1: What do we know?

Part 2: What's next?

Equation:

Solution:

Figure 7.46 Challenge Two-Step Word Problem Cards

Larry had 5 marbles. He had 2 more than Mike had. How many did they have altogether?

Part 1: What do we know?

Part 2: What's next?

Equation:

Solution:

Noelle had 8 marbles. She had 2 fewer than Mike had. How many did they have altogether?

Part 1: What do we know?

Part 2: What's next?

Equation:

Solution:

Kristi had 7 marbles. She had 2 fewer than Carole had. How many did they have altogether?

Part 1: What do we know?

Part 2: What's next?

Equation:

Solution:

Marcus had 7 marbles. He had 2 more than Luke had. How many did they have altogether?

Part 1: What do we know?

Part 2: What's next?

Equation:

Solution:

Marta had 10 marbles. She had 9 more than Dan had. How many did they have altogether?

Part 1: What do we know?

Part 2: What's next?

Equation:

Solution:

Cathy had 6 marbles. She had 4 fewer than Marta had. How many did they have altogether?

Part 1: What do we know?

Part 2: What's next?

Equation:

Solution:

Figure 7.47 Close

Close
◆ What did we do today?
◆ What was the math we were practicing?
◆ Was this easy or tricky?
◆ Turn to a partner and state one thing you learned today.

Abstract Lesson

Figure 7.48 Abstract Introduction

<table>
<tr>
<td colspan="2" align="center"><h2>Introduction</h2></td>
</tr>
<tr>
<td>Launch</td>
<td>
Teacher: Today we are going to continue to work on solving 2-step word problems. Here we have word problems on a card. Let's look at our math talk chart.

Vocabulary: take away, subtract, minus sign, plus sign, altogether, addend, compare, more than, fewer than, equation model

Math Talk: My model was….. First I …. Then I …..
</td>
</tr>
<tr>
<td>Model</td>
<td>
Teacher: So today we are going to do the 2-step word problem and we are going to model it now with the bar diagram. So instead of using the paper we are just going to draw the rectangles. What is important when thinking about the rectangles?

Juli: You have look at the size. If it is big then you have to make it big.

Teacher: Ok, if what's big?

Juli: The number.

Teacher: Ok, let's look at this problem:

Hugo: I know that Cathy had 7 and 1 less is 6 and 6 and 6 is 12. So 6 and 7 is 13.

<table>
<tr><td colspan="2">Cathy had 7 marbles. Marta had 1 less than she did. How many did they have altogether?</td></tr>
<tr><td colspan="2">Part 1: What do we know?

7 C
6 M   } ?</td></tr>
<tr><td colspan="2">Part 2: What's next?
Equation: $7 + 6 = 13$
Solution: 13 marbles</td></tr>
</table>
</td>
</tr>
<tr>
<td>Checking for Understanding</td>
<td>Teacher: Yes. I want you to read your problem and then decide which way you are going to model your problem. Each person is going to get a chance to do one and explain their thinking.</td>
</tr>
</table>

Figure 7.49 Student Activity

	<h2 style="text-align:center">Student Activity</h2>
Guided Practice/ Checking for Understanding	**Teacher:** Today we are going to work on word problems. You will pick a card and decide how you are going to solve your problem. **Marcos had 10 marbles. Kelly had 2 more than he did. How many did they have altogether?** **Part 1: What do we know?** M ⬜ 10 ⬜ K ⬜ ? ⬜ +2 ⬜ } ? **Part 2: What's next?** **Equation: 10 + 12 =22** **Solution: 22 marbles** **Teacher:** Who can describe his tape diagram? **Toddy:** He drew 10 and then the other one is a little longer because it said Kelly had 2 more.
Set up for Independent Practice	The teacher continues to watch the groups as they work on solving their problems. When everyone has finished the teacher asks the students to explain their thinking. She also asks them what was easy and what was tricky?

Figure 7.50 Close

<h2 style="text-align:center">Close</h2>
♦ What did we do today? ♦ What was the math we were practicing? ♦ Was this easy or tricky? ♦ Turn to a partner and state one thing you learned today.

Figure 7.51 Word Problem Cards

Kristi had 10 marbles. Mike had 3 fewer than she had. How many did they have altogether?
Part 1: What do we know?
Part 2: What's next? Equation: Solution:
Marcus had 10 marbles. He had 5 fewer than Luke had. How many did they have altogether?
Part 1: What do we know?
Part 2: What's next? Equation: Solution:
Lucia had 10 marbles. She had 8 more than Marta had. How many did they have altogether?
Part 1: What do we know?
Part 2: What's next? Equation: Solution:
Cathy had 19 marbles. Marta had 10. How many did they have altogether?
Part 1: What do we know?
Part 2: What's next? Equation: Solution:

Section Summary

Two-step problems can get tricky. The first types are easy but they gradually increase in difficulty. It is important to use easy numbers in the beginning. After the students are able to solve the problems, increase the number range. It is important that students slow down and unpack the problems, not depending on key words but on their understanding of what is taking place in the problem.

Measurement

Overview

Figure 7.52 Overview

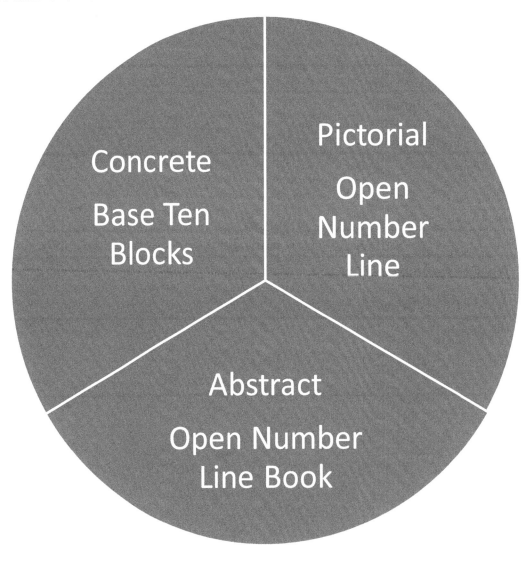

Figure 7.53 Planning Template

Measurement Word Problems

Big Idea: There are different types of word problems. Today we are going to model measurement word problems with the open number line. **Enduring Understanding:** We can model problems in many ways. **Essential Question:** What are the ways to model this type of problem? **I can statement:** I can model with an open number line.	**Materials** ♦ Tools: Cubes ♦ Templates: Ten Frame ♦ Cards ♦ Crayons
Cycle of Engagement **Concrete:** 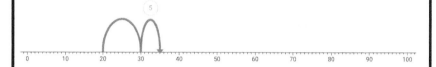 **Pictorial:** Drawing **Abstract:** Mental Number line 78 + 99 100 + 77	**Vocabulary & Language Frames** ♦ Count Up ♦ Count Back ♦ Addends ♦ Sum ♦ Difference

Figure 7.54 Differentiated Lessons

Three Differentiated Lessons In this series of lessons, students are working on the concept of *measurement problems*. They are developing this concept through concrete activities, pictorial activities, and abstract activities. Everybody should do the cycle. Some students progress through it more quickly than others. Here are some things to think about as you do these lessons.		
Emerging	**On Grade Level**	**Above Grade Level**
Make sure that students have a good understanding of the beaded and marked number line.	Students are introduced to the open number line in most states in second grade. The grade-level standard is that students can model it and explain it. So do lots of this work where students are modeling it and explaining it.	Extend the number range.
	In many states, this is a second-grade problem. For measurement problems, use measuring tapes, printable laminated yard sticks, and meter sticks.	

Figure 7.55 Anchor Chart

Solving Problems on the Open Number line

First, show it on the marked number line. This helps to scaffold students into using the open number line.

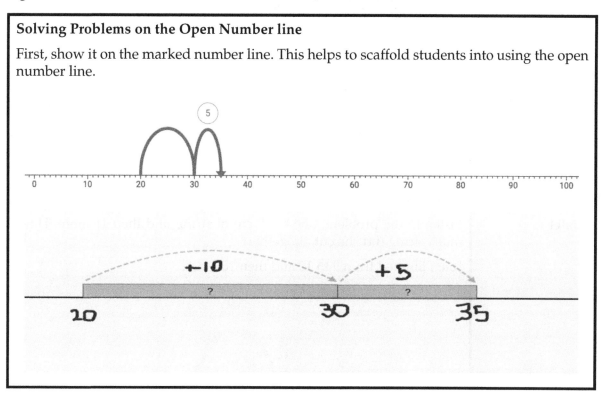

Concrete Lesson

Figure 7.56 Concrete Introduction

	Introduction
Launch	**Teacher:** Today we are going to work on looking at the open number line to solve problems. We have been working with this some in whole group.
	Vocabulary: compare, more, less, same as, word problem, count up, count back
Model	Listen to the problem. Sue cut 9 cm of string and then 11 more. How much string did she cut altogether?
	Jon: I jumped from 9 to 10 and then 10 more.
Checking for Understanding	**Teacher:** Who can show this problem: 29 + 21?
	The teacher reads two more problems that the group discusses.
	Teacher: Ok. I am going to give each one of you your own problem. I want you to read it. Solve it. Be ready to share how you did it. I am going to watch you and if you need help, look at our anchor charts and of course you can ask me.

Figure 7.57 Student Activity

	Student Activity
Guided Practice/ Checking for Understanding	The teacher passes out the problems. Students pull a card and act out their problems. The students each get a chance to share their problem and explain how they solved it. Students lay out the base ten blocks and then draw it out. **Kim: My problem is this:** Kelly used 25 cm of string to make bracelets. Then, she used 17 more cm of string. How much string did she use altogether? I drew the number line. I started at 25 and then added 20 more. Then I took away 3 because I had added 3 too many. I got 42 cm.
Set up for Independent Practice	*Every child shares out their problem and how they solved it.* **Teacher:** We are going to be talking more about this in the upcoming days. Are there any questions? What was interesting today? What was tricky?

Figure 7.58 Lesson Close

Close
♦ What did we do today? ♦ What was the math we were practicing? ♦ Was this easy or tricky? ♦ Turn to a partner and state one thing you learned today.

Figure 7.59 Cards

Kelly used 15 cm of string to make bracelets. Then, she used 10 more cm. How much did she use altogether?	Sue used 10 cm of string to make bracelets. Then she used 70 cm more. How much did she use altogether?
Sam jumped 50 cm and then 50 more. How far did she jump altogether?	Scott jumped 80 cm and then 60 more. How far did he jump altogether?
Kelly used 50 cm of string to make bracelets. Then, she used 40 more cm to make necklaces. How much string did she use altogether?	Sue used 20 cm of string to make bracelets. Then she used 60 cm more to make necklaces. How much did she use altogether?

Pictorial Lesson

Figure 7.60 Pictorial Introduction

<table>
<tr><td colspan="2" align="center"><h2>Introduction</h2></td></tr>
<tr>
<td>Launch</td>
<td>Teacher: Today we are going to work on solving measurement word problems with sketches.

Vocabulary: compare, more than, less than, equal to, same as, whole, word problem, count up, number sentence (equation)

Math Talk: My model was…. My strategy was ….</td>
</tr>
<tr>
<td>Model</td>
<td>Teacher: Kara used 50 cm to make bracelets. She also used 30 cm to make necklaces. How much string did she use altogether?

Teacher: We are going to use the open number line.

Ted: You jumped to 50 and then 30 more.

</td>
</tr>
<tr>
<td>Checking for Understanding</td>
<td>Teacher: Who wants to do one?

Marta: I want to try one.

Kayla jumped 72 cm. Then she jumped 28 more. How far did she jump?

I can go, 70 and then jump 20 more and then 10 more. See.

This conversation continues with the students practicing on the open beaded number line.</td>
</tr>
</table>

Figure 7.61 Student Activity

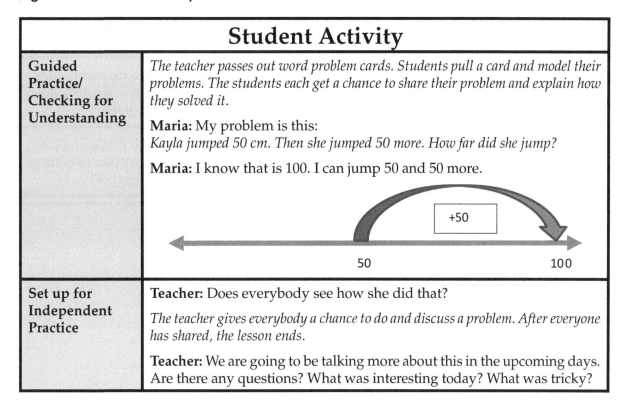

	Student Activity
Guided Practice/ Checking for Understanding	*The teacher passes out word problem cards. Students pull a card and model their problems. The students each get a chance to share their problem and explain how they solved it.* **Maria:** My problem is this: *Kayla jumped 50 cm. Then she jumped 50 more. How far did she jump?* **Maria:** I know that is 100. I can jump 50 and 50 more.
Set up for Independent Practice	**Teacher:** Does everybody see how she did that? *The teacher gives everybody a chance to do and discuss a problem. After everyone has shared, the lesson ends.* **Teacher:** We are going to be talking more about this in the upcoming days. Are there any questions? What was interesting today? What was tricky?

Figure 7.62 Lesson Close

Close

♦ What did we do today?

♦ What was the math we were practicing?

♦ Was this easy or tricky?

♦ Turn to a partner and state one thing you learned today.

Figure 7.63 Cards

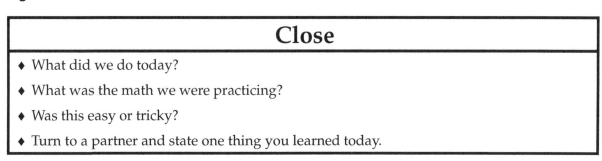

Kelly used 10 cm of string to make bracelets. Then, she used 10 more cm. How much did she use altogether?	Sue used 10 cm of string to make bracelets. Then she used 20 cm more. How much did she use altogether?
Sam jumped 50 cm and then 40 more. How far did she jump altogether?	Scott jumped 80 cm and then 20 more. How far did he jump altogether?

Kelly used 10 cm of string to make bracelets. Then, she used 10 more cm. How much did she use altogether?	Sue used 10 cm of string to make bracelets. Then she used 20 cm more. How much did she use altogether?
Kelly used 50 cm of string to make bracelets. Then, she used 50 more cm to make necklaces. How much string did she use altogether?	Sue used 20 cm of string to make bracelets. Then she used 30 cm more to make necklaces. How much did she use altogether?
Kelly used 75 cm of string to make bracelets. Then, she used 25 more cm to make necklaces. How much string did she use altogether?	Sue used 75 cm of string to make bracelets. Then she used 10 cm more to make necklaces. How much did she use altogether?

Abstract Lesson

Figure 7.64 Abstract Introduction

<table>
<tr><td colspan="3"><h2 style="text-align:center">Introduction</h2></td></tr>
<tr>
<td>Launch</td>
<td colspan="2">Teacher: Today we are going to continue to work on solving word problems on the open number line. Let's look at our math talk chart:

Vocabulary: take away, subtract, minus sign, plus sign, altogether, addend, compare, more than, fewer than, equation model

Teacher: We are going to do an activity where you write an open number line book. There are several pages. You are going to start working on your book in our group, but you will continue working on it in the workstation.</td>
</tr>
<tr>
<td rowspan="4">Model</td>
<td>My Open Number Line Book</td>
<td>An open number line is

I can model different types of word problems with my open number line.</td>
</tr>
<tr>
<td>I can jump by tens on the open number line.</td>
<td>I can add tens and 1's on the open number line.</td>
</tr>
<tr>
<td>I can jump tens and ones.</td>
<td>I can add 3 numbers on the open number line.</td>
</tr>
<tr>
<td>I can add 4 numbers on the open number line.</td>
<td>Here is my very own word problem that I am going to solve on the open number line.</td>
</tr>
<tr>
<td>Checking for Understanding</td>
<td colspan="2">Teacher: Who can tell me what we are going to do?

Tiffany: We are going to make a book about using the open number lines.

Dan: We write our own examples.</td>
</tr>
</table>

Figure 7.65 Student Activity

<table>
<tr><td colspan="2"><h2 style="text-align:center">Student Activity</h2></td></tr>
<tr>
<td>Guided Practice/ Checking for Understanding</td>
<td>Teacher: Everybody start on whatever page you want. We will share out in a little while.

    I can jump by tens on the open number line.

</td>
</tr>
</table>

Set up for Independent Practice	The teacher continues to watch the groups as they work on solving their problems. When everyone has finished the teacher asks the students to explain their thinking. She also asks them what was easy and what was tricky.

Figure 7.66 Lesson Close

Close

♦ What did we do today?

♦ What was the math we were practicing?

♦ Was this easy or tricky?

♦ Turn to a partner and state one thing you learned today.

Figure 7.67 Cards

My Open Number Line Book	An open number line is I can model different types of word problems with my open number line.
I can jump by tens on the open number line.	I can add tens and ones on the open number line.
I can jump tens and ones.	I can add three numbers on the open number line.
I can add four numbers on the open number line.	Here is my very own word problem that I am going to solve on the open number line.

Section Summary

Open number lines are tricky. They are highly dependent on students' understanding of the number line. Too often students are rushed into using them. They should explore them and play around with them. They should be familiar with the beaded number line and the marked number line. They should have a strong sense of the relative magnitude of number. They should be allowed to fiddle around with the open number line using place value blocks, so that they can begin to make meaning of the problems and how to use the number line. If you take the time to do all of this, then students really enjoy using open number lines.

3-Read Problems

Figure 7.68 Planning Template

3-Read Problems

Big Idea: We can use different strategies and models to solve word problems. **Enduring Understanding:** We can model problems in many ways. **Essential Question:** What are the ways to model this type of problem? **I can statement:** I can use tools to model my thinking.	**Materials** ♦ Tools: Cubes ♦ Templates: Ten Frame ♦ Cards ♦ Crayons
Cycle of Engagement **Concrete–Pictorial–Abstract:** In this type of problem, the class chorally reads the problem three times. The first time the class reads the problem, they focus on what is happening in the problem. The second time, they focus on what the numbers mean. The third time, they focus on asking questions about the problems.	**Vocabulary & Language Frames** Strategies Models Tools

Figure 7.69 3-Read Word Problem

3-Read Word Problem

We can read a problem three times.

The first time we read it and think about the situation.

What is the story about? Who is in it? What is happening?

The second time we read it and think about the numbers.

What are the numbers? What do they mean? What might we do with those numbers in this situation?

The third time we read it and think about what questions we could ask.

What do we notice in this story? What do we wonder? What do we want to ask about this story?

The Jones family went on vacation. They drove 25 miles on Monday. They drove 50 miles on Tuesday. They drove 20 miles on Wednesday.

First Read: *What is this story about?* It is about a family who went on vacation.

Second Read: *What do the numbers mean?* They tell us how far they drove. On Monday they drove 25 miles. On Tuesday they drove 50 miles and on Wednesday they drove 20 miles.

Third Read: *What could we ask about this story?*

How far did they drive altogether?

How much farther did they drive on Monday than on Tuesday?

How many fewer miles did they drive on Wednesday than they drove on Tuesday?

Figure 7.70 3-Read Word Problems Lesson

3-Read Word Problems Lesson

Teacher: Today we are going to work on word problems. We are going to do a 3-read, like the ones we do in whole group.

Vocabulary: model, strategy

Story: The bakery had 15 cookies. They had 17 chocolate chip, 14 peanut butter, and 15 lemon ones.

First Read: *What is this story about?*

It is about the bakery. They have 3 different types of cookies.

Second Read: *What do the numbers mean?*

They have 17 chocolate chip cookies, 14 peanut butter cookies, and 15 lemon ones.

Third Read: *What could we ask about this story?*

How many cookies were there altogether?

How many more chocolate chip cookies did they have than peanut butter ones?

How many fewer lemon cookies did they have than chocolate chip cookies?

Teacher: Ok, pick two questions and answer them. We will come back in a few minutes to discuss them. . . . Who answered question 1? Tell us your strategy and show us a model of your thinking.

Timothy: I did how many do they have altogether? I added it up on the rekenrek.

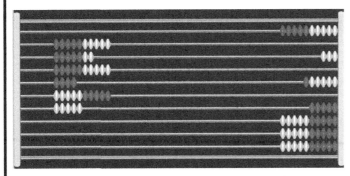

www.didax.com/apps/100-bead-rekenrek/

I added the tens and then the ones. So I got 30 and then 9 and 7 which is 16. I got 46.

Teacher: Ok, who did question 2?

Eric: I did how many more chocolate chip cookies than peanut butter ones. I used the number path. I see that there are 3 more chocolate chip cookies.

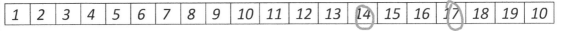

1	2	3	4	5	6	7	8	9	10	11	12	13	14	15	16	17	18	19	10

Students continue to share their thinking with the group. When they are done, the teacher facilitates a conversation about what the math was for the day and then what students thought was easy and what they thought was tricky.

Figure 7.71 Close

Close
♦ What did we do today?
♦ What was the math we were practicing?
♦ Was this easy or tricky?
♦ Turn to a partner and state one thing you learned today.

Figure 7.72 3-Read Cards

The teacher had 10 pencils. 15 were blue and 4 were green and 11 were yellow.	Terri biked 2 miles on Wednesday, 12 miles on Thursday, and 13 miles on Friday.
Marta had 16 red marbles, 20 orange marbles, and 25 blue marbles.	The store had 20 red apples, 30 green apples, and 50 yellow apples.
Kelly had 24 blue rings, 24 orange rings, and 1 pink ring.	Grandma made fruit punch. She used 10 apples, 14 oranges, and 6 pineapples.
Grandma made fruit punch. She used 25 apples, 35 peaches, and 5 oranges.	Grandma made some pies. She made 14 apple, 5 lemon, and 6 cherry.
The jewelry store had 15 bracelets, 7 rings, and 3 necklaces.	Sharon had 9 red rings, 8 blue rings, and 7 purple rings.

Picture Prompts

Figure 7.73 Planning Template

Picture Prompt Word Problems

Big Idea: Word problems are a part of our everyday lives. **Enduring Understanding:** We can model problems in many ways. There are many different strategies to solve them. **Essential Question:** What are the ways to model problems? **I can statement:** I can model problems.	**Materials** ♦ Tools: Cubes ♦ Templates: Ten Frame ♦ Cards ♦ Crayons
	Questions ♦ What is your strategy? ♦ What is your model? ♦ Why does that work? ♦ How can you show that?
Cycle of Engagement **Concrete:** **Pictorial:** Drawing **Abstract:** Equations $2 + ? = 8$	**Vocabulary & Language Frames** My strategy was . . . My model was . . .

Figure 7.74 Picture Prompt Word Problem Lesson

Picture Prompt Word Problems

Teacher: Today we are going to look at pictures and tell word problems. We are working mainly on addition and subtraction stories. Here is a picture. This is my story. The bakery had 4 rows of donuts with 5 donuts in each column.

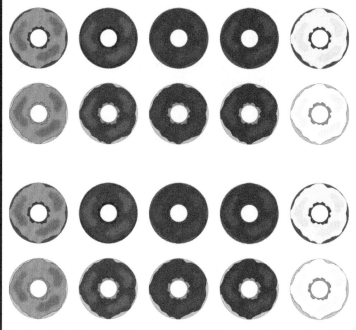

Luke: That's easy. There were 20 donuts altogether. My equation is 4 + 4 + 4 + 4 + 4.

Teacher: Ok, that works! Who can tell a different story?

Marta: There was a basket of 20 donuts. 9 were pink. The rest were other colors.

Kelly: That's easy. 11 because 9 and 11 are 20. See? (*She points to the number line.*)

Teacher: Ok. Who's next?

The teacher goes around the circle and everyone gets a chance to share their stories. They then wrap up and go to workstations.

Figure 7.75 Open Word Problems

> **Open Word Problems Lesson**
>
> **Teacher:** Today we are going to work on word problems.
>
> **Vocabulary:** model, strategy, tool, sum, difference, addend
>
> **Math Talk:** The sum is _____. The difference is _____.
>
> **Teacher:** The answer is 40 strawberries. What is the question?
>
> **Terry:** I know. There were 20 regular strawberries. There were 20 chocolate-covered strawberries. How many strawberries were there altogether?
>
> **Kayla:** 40.
>
> **Kayla:** Ok, I got one. There were 50 chocolate-covered strawberries and Maite ate 10. (*They all giggle because Maite is at the table.*) How many were left?
>
> **Maite:** 10 no no no, I mean 40.
>
> *The students continue telling stories where the answer is 40. They have plenty of tools on the table, including a rekenrek, empty and filled hundred grids, and twenty frame counters. After they finish, the teacher asks them what they were doing and if it was easy or tricky. Then, the students are released back to continue their menu work.*

Section Summary

It is important to do open questions with students where they have to contextualize numbers. This is part of the mathematical practices and processes (National Governors Association Center for Best Practices & Council of Chief State School; NCTM, 2000). We want students to be able to reason about numbers. We want students to be able to tell stories about addition and subtraction. Giving them rich structures to do that is vital.

Depth of Knowledge

Depth of Knowledge is a framework that encourages us to ask questions that require that students think, reason, explain, defend, and justify their thinking (Webb, 2002). Figures 7.76 and 7.77 are a snapshot of what that can look like in terms of place value work.

A great resource for asking open questions is Marion Small's *Good Questions: Great Ways to Differentiate Mathematics Instruction in the Standards-Based Classroom* (2017).

Also, Robert Kaplinsky has done a great job in pushing our thinking forward with the Depth of Knowledge Matrices he created (https://robertkaplinsky.com/depth-knowledge-matrix-elementary-math/). Kentucky Math Department (2007) has these great math matrices as well.

Figure 7.76 DOK Activities

	What are different strategies and models that we can use to solve start unknown problems?	What are different strategies and models to solve two-step word problems?	What are different strategies and models that we can use to model measurement problems on the open number line?
DOK Level 1 (These are questions where students are required to simply recall/reproduce an answer/do a procedure.)	Solve. Sue had some rings. She got 5 more. Now she has 12. How many did she have in the beginning?	Solve with manipulatives. Write the equation. Jamal had 12 marbles. His brother had 10 more than he had. How many did they have altogether?	Solve the measurement word problem on the open number line. Use the base ten blocks to show your thinking. Sue jumped 26 inches and then another 32 inches. How far did she jump altogether?
DOK Level 2 (These are questions where students have to use information, think about concepts and reason.) This is considered a more challenging problem than a level 1 problem.	Solve in two different ways. Explain your thinking. Sue had some rings. She got 5 more. Now she has 12. How many did she have in the beginning?	Solve with a math sketch. Write the set-up equation and the solution equation. Explain your thinking. Jamal had 12 marbles. His brother had 10 more than he had. How many did they have altogether?	Solve the measurement word problem on the open number line. Explain your thinking. Sue jumped 26 inches and then another 32 inches. How far did she jump altogether?

	What are different strategies and models that we can use to solve start unknown problems?	What are different strategies and models to solve two-step word problems?	What are different strategies and models that we can use to model measurement problems on the open number line?
DOK Level 3 (These are questions where students have to reason, plan, explain, justify, and defend their thinking.)	Solve. Sue had some rings. She got ___ more. Now she has __. How many did she have in the beginning? Defend your answer. Prove that it is correct by solving one way and checking another.	Solve. Write the set-up equation and the solution equation. Jamal had 12 marbles. His brother had 10 more than he had. How many did they have altogether? Defend your answer. Prove that it is correct by solving one way and checking another.	Make up a measurement word problem and solve it on the number line. Defend your thinking. Prove that you are correct.

Figure 7.77 Asking rigorous questions

DOK 1	DOK 2 At this level, students explain their thinking.	DOK 3 At this level, students have to justify, defend, and prove their thinking with objects, drawings, and diagrams.
What is the answer to . . . ? Can you model the problem? Can you identify the answer that matches this equation?	How do you know that the equation is correct? Can you pick the correct answer and explain why it is correct? How can you model that problem in more than one way? What is another way to model that problem? Can you model that on the . . . ? Give me an example of a . . . type of problem . . . Which answer is incorrect? Explain your thinking.	Can you prove that your answer is correct? Prove that . . . Explain why that is the answer. . . . Show me how to solve that and explain what you are doing. Defend your thinking.

Key Points

♦ Start Unknown Problems
♦ Part-Part Whole
♦ Compare
♦ Two-Step
♦ Picture Prompts
♦ 3-Read Problems
♦ Open Word Problems

Summary

It is important to work with students in small guided math groups focusing on word problems. Word problems have a learning trajectory (Carpenter et al., 1999/2015). Most states have outlined the word problem types that each grade level is responsible for in their standards. So in a guided math group, the goal is to work with students around the word problem types that they are learning.

Students are usually at different levels when learning word problems. They are scaffolded into a hierarchy that goes from easy to challenging. In most states, first-grade students are responsible for about 11 of the 15 add/subtraction problem types. In some states (like Texas), they are responsible for all the problem types. By second grade, students are supposed to understand all the 15 traditional problem types and the five different types of two-step problems.

The small-group discussion should reference the whole-group problem-solving work. The focus should be on getting students to think about the context and the numbers, to reason about the problem, and to use visual representations and tools to unpack it. Students should have to write an equation with a symbol for the unknown and solve one way and check another. Problem solving should be done throughout the year, in different parts of Math Workshop, during the introduction, in math workstations, sometimes in guided math groups, and sometimes for homework.

Reflection Questions

1. How are you currently teaching word problem lessons?
2. Are you making sure that you do concrete, pictorial, and abstract activities?
3. What do your students struggle with the most and what ideas are you taking away from this chapter that might inform your work around those struggles?

References

Carpenter, T. P., Fennema, E., Franke, M. L., Levi, L., & Empson, S. B. (1999/2015). *Children's mathematics: Cognitively guided instruction*. Portsmouth, NH: Heinemann.

Cummins, D. D., Kintsch, W., Reusser, K., & Weimer, R. (1988). The role of understanding in solving word problems. *Cognitive Psychology*, 20(4), 405–438.

Fuchs, L. S., Zumeta, R. O., Schumacher, R. F., Powell, S. R., Seethaler, P. M., Hamlett, C. L., & Fuchs, D. (2010). The effects of schema-broadening instruction on second graders' word-problem performance and their ability to represent word problems with algebraic equations: A randomized control study. *The Elementary School Journal, 110*, 440–463.

Jitendra, A. K., Hoff, K., & Beck, M. M. (1999). Teaching middle school students with learning disabilities to solve word problems using a schema-based approach. *Remedial and Special Education, 20*, 50–64.

Kentucky Department of Education (2007). Support Materials for Core Content for Assessment Version 4.1 Mathematics. Retrieved from the internet on January 15th, 2017.

National Governors Association Center for Best Practices & Council of Chief State School Officers. (2010). *Common core state standards for mathematics*. Washington, DC: Authors.

National Council of Teachers of Mathematics. (2000). Principles and standards for school mathematics. Reston, VA: National Council of Teachers of Mathematics.

Schoenfeld, A. H. (1991). On mathematics as sense-making: An informal attack on the unfortunate divorce of formal and informal mathematics. In J. F. Voss, D. N. Perkins, & J. W. Segal (Eds.), *Informal reasoning and education* (pp. 311–343). Hillsdale, NJ: Lawrence Erlbaum Associates.

Smalls, M. (2009). *Good questions: Great ways to differentiate mathematics instructions*. New York: TC Press.

Smalls, M. (2017). *Good questions: Great ways to differentiate mathematics instructions* (3rd ed.). New York, NY: TC Press.

Stacey, K., & MacGregor, M. (1999). Learning the algebraic method of solving problems. *The Journal of Mathematical Behavior, 18*(2), 149–167. doi:10.1016/S0732-3123(99)00026-7

Verschaffel, L., Greer, B., & De Corte, E. (2000). *Making sense of word problems*. Lisse, The Netherlands: Swets & Zeitlinger.

Webb, N. (2002). *An analysis of the alignment between mathematics standards and assessments for three states*. Paper presented at the annual meeting of the American educational Research Association, New Orleans, LA.

8
Place Value Guided Math Lessons

Second-grade place value is extremely important. It not only solidifies initial understandings from kindergarten and first grade, it also teaches new standards so that by the end of second grade students in most states have been introduced to 15 to 17 topics on place value. The research clearly confirms that place value is very important (National Council of Teachers of Mathematics, 2000; Sherman, Richardson, & Yard, 2013). Researchers have found that a strong understanding of place value has a positive impact on later mathematics achievement (Miura, Okamoto, Chungsoon, & Steere, 1993; Moeller, Pixner, Zuber, Kaufmann, & Nuerk, 2011). In these lessons, we explore how to build an understanding of place value along the learning trajectory so that students understand what it looks like and feels like and how to use it to understand and work with numbers.

Students should have plenty of opportunities to practice the big ideas concretely, pictorially, and abstractly. Students should have plenty of opportunities to use various tools to explore the concepts. The concepts are the foundation of our math system. Too often, students are rushed through a place value chapter and then the concepts are never addressed again. Place value should be interwoven throughout the year, and it should stay up as a workstation center. The National Council of Teachers of Mathematics (NCTM, 2000) notes that students should "use multiple models to develop initial understandings of place value and the base-ten number system."

I want to emphasize that you should use not only place value blocks but also rekenreks, beaded number lines, base ten paper, and sketches. Cuisenaire™ rods and digiblocks are also great tools to use. The idea is that the more ways that students can think about and explore the concept, the more opportunities they have to own it and make sense of it in different ways. The research says that the more ways that students can model concepts the better their understanding. The sample guided math lessons in this chapter take the student through the cycle of concrete, pictorial, and abstract to teach:

♦ Representing 3-digit numbers
♦ Adding two 2-digit numbers
♦ Adding 10 to a number
♦ Comparing numbers

Research Note 🔍

♦ A good foundation in place value is essential (National Council of Teachers of Mathematics, 2000; National Research Council, 2009).

♦ Research consistently finds that students struggle with place and have difficulty understanding tens and ones (Hanich, Jordan, Kaplan, & Dick, 2001; Jordan & Hanich, 2000; Kamii, 1985; Kamii & Joseph, 1988).

♦ The National Council of Teachers of Mathematics (NCTM, 2000, in their Number and Operations Standards for Grades Pre-K-2) states that students should "use multiple models to develop initial understandings of place value and the base-ten number system.".

Figure 8.1 Overview

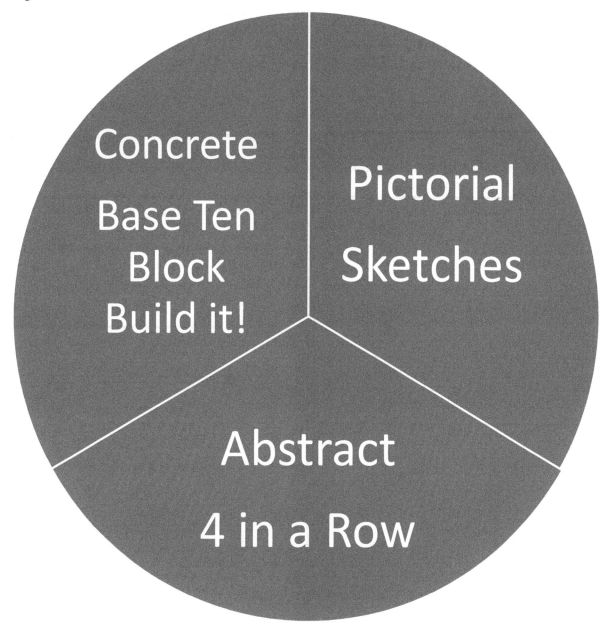

Figure 8.2 Planning Template

Grouping Hundreds, Tens, and Ones

Big Idea: We can break up numbers into hundreds, tens, and ones.

Enduring Understanding: Students will understand that our system is based on groups of tens and ones.

Essential Question: What are the ways to model tens and ones?

I can statement: I can break apart a number into hundreds, tens, and ones.

Materials
♦ Tools: Cubes
♦ Templates: Ten Frame
♦ Cards
♦ Crayons

Cycle of Engagement

Concrete:
INSERT
Pictorial: Drawing

Vocabulary & Language Frames

Vocabulary: add, sum, addend, plus, equals, makes, tens, ones, hundreds
Math Talk: I have ____ hundreds and ___ tens and ____ones. I have _____.

Abstract: 200 Hundred Grid

1	2	3	4	5	6	7	8	9	10
11	12	13	14	15	16	17	18	19	20
21	22	23	24	25	26	27	28	29	30
31	32	33	34	35	36	37	38	39	40
41	42	43	44	45	46	47	48	49	50
51	52	53	54	55	56	57	58	59	60
61	62	63	64	65	66	67	68	69	70
71	72	73	74	75	76	77	78	79	80
81	82	83	84	85	86	87	88	89	90
91	92	93	94	95	96	97	98	99	100
101	102	103	104	105	106	107	108	109	110
111	112	113	114	115	116	117	118	119	120
121	122	123	124	125	126	127	128	129	130
131	132	133	134	135	136	137	138	139	140
141	142	143	144	145	146	147	148	149	150
151	152	153	154	155	156	157	158	159	160
161	162	163	164	165	166	167	168	169	170
171	172	173	174	175	176	177	178	179	180
181	182	183	184	185	186	187	188	189	190
191	192	193	194	195	196	197	198	199	200

Figure 8.3 Differentiation

Three Differentiated Lessons

In this series of lessons, students are working on the concept of *composing and decomposing 2- and 3-digit numbers*. They are developing this concept through concrete activities, pictorial activities, and abstract activities. Here are some things to think about as you do these lessons.

Emerging	On Grade Level	Above Grade Level
Do a lot of work with students building the hundreds, tens, and ones on bean sticks, with straws, and with cubes.	Do a lot of work on building tens and ones and then transition sooner to place value blocks.	Work with larger numbers.

 Looking for Misunderstandings and Common Errors

Students have trouble with the language of place value. Be sure to do activities and energizers where you unpack the language. For example, students will write two hundred five like this: 2005. So it is important to work with the actual place and value of numbers.

Figure 8.4 Anchor Chart

122
Base Ten Blocks

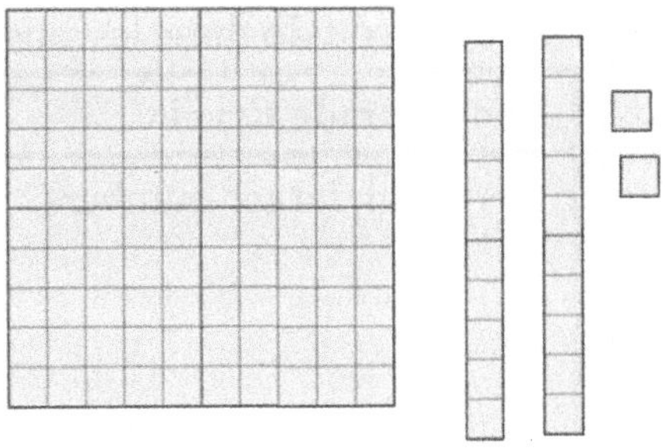

Cube Counting Paper

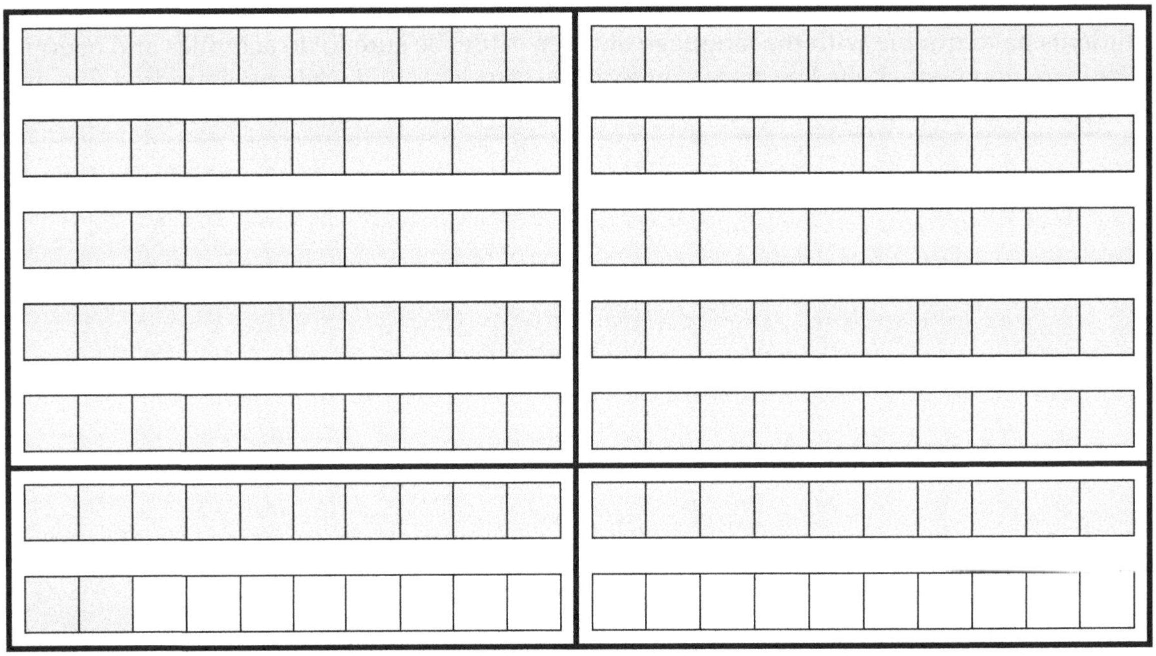

Sketch

Concrete Lesson

Figure 8.5 Concrete Introduction

Introduction

Anchor Activity: Concrete Lesson With Place Value Blocks Connecting With Sketches and Abstract Numeral

Launch	**Vocabulary:** add, sum, addend, plus, equals, makes, tens, ones, hundreds **Math Talk:** I have ____ hundreds and ___tens and ____ones. I have _____. **Teacher:** Today we are going to work on breaking apart numbers into hundreds, tens, and ones. We have the base ten blocks. If I have the number 105, what could that look like if we broke it into hundreds, tens, and ones. **Claire:** There is 1 hundred, no tens, and 5 ones.
Model	**Teacher:** Let's look at how we might write that. $100 + 0 + 5$ **Teacher:** Let's do another one. What about 147? **Tom:** There is 1 hundred, 4 tens, and 7 ones.
Checking for Understanding	**Teacher:** Who wants to try and write that out in what we call "expanded form" because we are "expanding it out"? **Maria:** $100 + 40 + 7$ **Teacher:** Ok. I am going to give each one of you a number. I want you to read it. I want you to build it and then write it in expanded form. Then, you will explain what you did to the group.

Figure 8.6 Student Activity

	Student Activity
Guided Practice/ Checking for Understanding	The teacher passes out the problems. Students go around and share their work. **Carole:** I have 135. I built it. 1 hundred, 3 tens, and 5 ones. 100 + 30 + 5. <table><tr><td>Hundreds</td><td>Tens</td><td>Ones</td></tr><tr><td></td><td></td><td></td></tr><tr><td>100 + 30 + 5</td><td></td><td></td></tr></table>
Set Up for Independent Practice	*Every child shares out their problem and how they solved it.* **Teacher:** We are going to be talking more about this in the upcoming days. Are there any questions? What was interesting today? What was tricky?

Figure 8.7 Lesson Close

Close
♦ What did we do today? ♦ What was the math we were practicing? ♦ Was this easy or tricky? ♦ Turn to a partner and state one thing you learned today.

Figure 8.8 Calling Cards

422	333	601	599	245
780	876	492	801	359
905	189	505	900	588
222	275	684	1000	702
127	382	732	157	951

Figure 8.9 Place Value Mat

Pictorial Lesson

Figure 8.10 Pictorial Introduction

<table>
<tr>
<td colspan="2" align="center">

Introduction

Representing Numbers With Math Sketches Connecting to Place Value Blocks and Expanded Form

</td>
</tr>
<tr>
<td>Launch</td>
<td>

Vocabulary: add, sum, addend, plus, equals, makes, tens, ones, hundreds

Math Talk: I have ____ hundreds and ___tens and ____ones. I have _____.

Teacher: Today we are going to continue counting hundreds, tens, and ones. We are going to use our white boards. I am going to tell you to sketch out a specific type of number. You have to sketch it, hold it up, and explain it to the group. You can build it first with the base ten blocks if you want to.

</td>
</tr>
<tr>
<td>Model</td>
<td>

Teacher: Sketch a number between 120 and 170.

Sara: I sketched 125. It has 1 hundred, 2 tens, and 5 ones.

Clark: I made 150 because 50 has 5 tens.

</td>
</tr>
<tr>
<td>Checking for Understanding</td>
<td>

Teacher: I am going to give each one of you an equation. I want you to practice representing it with your sketches and write the number in expanded form. Then, you will explain what you did and what the equation is. Who wants to go first?

</td>
</tr>
</table>

Figure 8.11 Student Activity

Student Activity	
Guided Practice/ Checking for Understanding	The teacher passes out cards with equations. Students pull a card and represent their thinking. The students each get a chance to share their problem and explain how they solved it. **Teacher:** Sketch out a number that is less than 159 but greater than 139. Now you have to think about that. Look at the 200 grid if you need to. **Marta:** I sketched 151 is less than 159 and greater than 139. **Teacher:** Who agrees with Marta? Is she correct? If so, explain why. **Dan:** I agree with Marta because it is greater than 139 and less than 159.
Set Up for Independent Practice	*The teacher gives everybody a chance to do and discuss a problem. After everyone has shared, the lesson ends.* **Teacher:** We are going to be talking more about this in the upcoming days. Are there any questions? What was interesting today? What was tricky?

Figure 8.12 Lesson Close

Close
♦ What did we do today? ♦ What was the math we were practicing? ♦ Was this easy or tricky? ♦ Turn to a partner and state one thing you learned today.

Figure 8.13 Sketch Cards

a number greater than 200	a number greater than 550	a number greater than 799
a number less than 200	a number less than 200	a number less than 200
a number in between 222 and 333	a number in between 59 and 107	a number in between 704 and 825
a number greater than _____	a number less than _____	a number in between _____
a number in between 709 and 724	a number in between 159 and 167	a number in between 432 and 523
a number close to 120	a number far from 503	a number near 888

Abstract Lesson

Figure 8.14 Abstract Introduction

Working With Expanded Form

Anchor Activity: Connect 4 Game (Mainly Abstract)

Launch	**Vocabulary:** add, sum, addend, plus, equals, makes, tens, ones, hundreds **Math Talk:** I have ____ hundreds and ___ tens and ____ ones. I have _____. **Teacher:** Today we are going to play four in a row. I am going to call out a number by expanded form and you have to cover it. Whoever covers it up and down, across or diagonally first wins.
Model	1 hundred, 4 tens, and 5 ones • 100 + 20 + 7 • 200 + 30 + 3 Five hundred seventy-three • 7 tens / 3 ones / 5 hundreds
Checking for Understanding	**Teacher:** On your board, if you have 145 you could cover it. If you have 127 you could cover it. If you have 233 you could cover it. You have to listen carefully to how many hundreds, tens, and ones though. It can be tricky. Ready? Any questions?

Figure 8.15 Student Activity

Student Activity	
Guided Practice/ Checking for Understanding	**Teacher:** Ok. Here is a card for each of you. You can win up and down, all the way across, or four corners.

125	233	344	159
261	377	489	599
614	770	855	972
181	293	335	427

112	215	316	477
552	830	245	157
631	942	399	201
788	126	455	144

433	127	218	322
153	631	744	856
899	979	181	222
111	316	465	155

399	123	219	417
454	532	649	750
931	825	743	154
177	246	375	180

The teacher calls out various numbers by hundreds, tens, and ones. Students listen and cover the numbers on their board.

Set Up for Inde- pendent Practice	**Teacher:** This week during your workstation activity, you will play this game in pairs with your partner. Pull a card. Cover that number. Whoever gets four in a row first wins.

Figure 8.16 Lesson Close

Close
◆ What did we do today? ◆ What was the math we were practicing? ◆ What were we doing with our number wands? ◆ Was this easy or tricky? ◆ Turn to a partner and state one thing you learned today.

Figure 8.17 Bingo Calling cards

1 hundred, 2 tens, and 5 ones	200 + 60 + 1	600 + 10 + 4
2 hundreds, 6 tens, and 1 one	100 + 50 + 9	200 + 90 + 3
3 hundreds, 7 tens, and 7 ones	500 + 90 + 9	900 + 70 + 2
2 hundreds, 3 tens, and 3 ones	100 + 80 + 1	200 + 30 + 3
3 hundreds, 3 tens, and 5 ones	400 + 80 + 9	100 + 10 + 1
8 hundreds, 5 tens, and 5 ones	400 + 20 + 7	200 + 30 + 3

Figure 8.18 Bingo Boards

125	233	344	159
261	377	489	599
614	770	855	972
181	293	335	427

427	855	489	181
377	344	125	614
293	599	261	233
770	159	335	972

233	159	377	599
770	181	335	972
293	855	427	614
489	261	344	125

181	377	855	233
427	261	770	125
972	344	489	614
159	335	293	599

Section Summary

When working with hundreds, tens, and ones, it is important to have students build it, draw it, and then match it. It is also really important to have students name a number in many different ways. For example, they should name 178 as 17 tens and 8 ones but also as 1 hundred, 7 tens, and 8 ones or as 178 ones, etc. You want to build flexibility around number. They should do number mats where they write a number and build and sketch it many different ways. Also, in the beginning have the students build bean sticks for tens and ones, so they get the idea of a ten. Have them do race to 200 games where they have to keep making exchanges of ones, tens, and hundreds to get to 200. The point is to provide many opportunities for students to work with hundreds, tens, and ones throughout the year, not only in the place value unit of study.

Figure 8.19 Overview

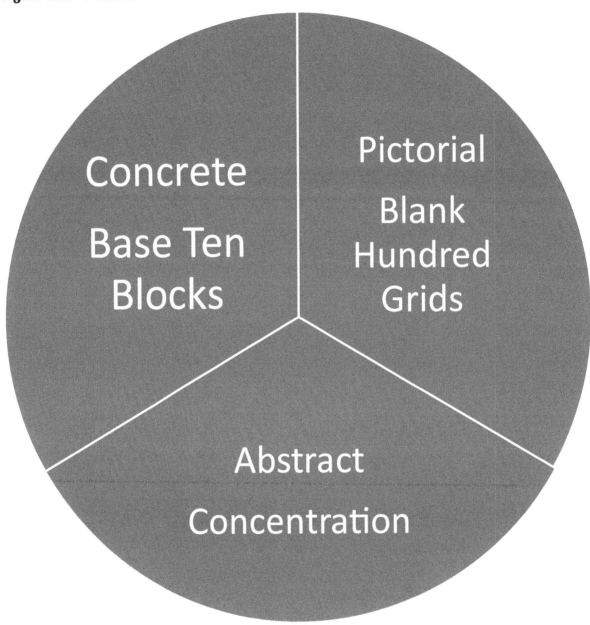

Figure 8.20 Planning Template

Adding 10 More to a Number

Big Idea: Using place value you can add 10 more to a number mentally. **Enduring Understanding:** We can model problems in many ways. **Essential Question:** What are the ways to model this type of problem? **I can statement:** I can model adding 10 to a number.	**Materials** ♦ Tools: Beaded Number Lines ♦ Templates: Ten Frame ♦ Cards ♦ Crayons
Cycle of Engagement **Concrete:** **Pictorial:** Drawing 	**Vocabulary & Language Frames** ♦ Count Up ♦ Addends ♦ _____ plus 10 makes _____. **Abstract:** $219 + 10 = 229$

Figure 8.21 Differentiation

Three Differentiated Lessons
In this series of lessons, students are working on the concept of *adding 10 more*. They are developing this concept through concrete activities, pictorial activities, and abstract activities. Here are some things to think about as you do these lessons.

Emerging	On Grade Level	Above Grade Level
Do a lot of work with students adding tens to 2- and 3-digit numbers with place value blocks. Review adding 2-digit numbers first.	The grade-level standard is that students can add 10 and 100 to 2- and 3-digit numbers. Work through the cycle of concrete, pictorial, and abstract representations.	Work with larger numbers.

 Looking for Misunderstandings and Common Errors

Students have a great deal of trouble adding tens. When they do vertical problems, they wiil line up the numbers incorrectly. Do a lot of work with base ten blocks and sketches before just doing straight computations.

Figure 8.22 Anchor Chart

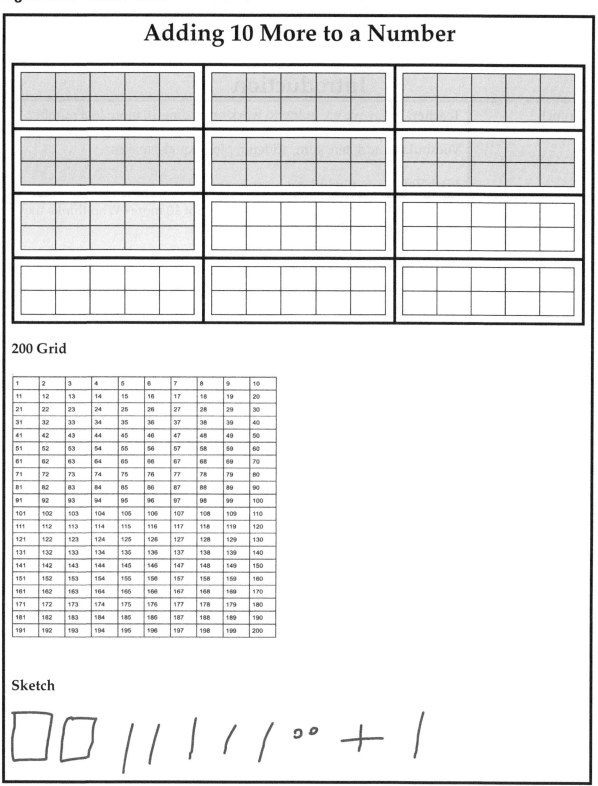

Adding 10 More to a Number

200 Grid

1	2	3	4	5	6	7	8	9	10
11	12	13	14	15	16	17	18	19	20
21	22	23	24	25	26	27	28	29	30
31	32	33	34	35	36	37	38	39	40
41	42	43	44	45	46	47	48	49	50
51	52	53	54	55	56	57	58	59	60
61	62	63	64	65	66	67	68	69	70
71	72	73	74	75	76	77	78	79	80
81	82	83	84	85	86	87	88	89	90
91	92	93	94	95	96	97	98	99	100
101	102	103	104	105	106	107	108	109	110
111	112	113	114	115	116	117	118	119	120
121	122	123	124	125	126	127	128	129	130
131	132	133	134	135	136	137	138	139	140
141	142	143	144	145	146	147	148	149	150
151	152	153	154	155	156	157	158	159	160
161	162	163	164	165	166	167	168	169	170
171	172	173	174	175	176	177	178	179	180
181	182	183	184	185	186	187	188	189	190
191	192	193	194	195	196	197	198	199	200

Sketch

Concrete Lesson

Figure 8.23 Concrete Introduction

	Introduction
Launch	**Teacher:** Today we are going to work on adding 10 more to a number. **Vocabulary:** add, ten, sum, addend, plus, equals, makes **Math Talk:** _____ plus 10 is _____.
Model	**Teacher:** What if I had 120 marbles and I got 10 more? Who thinks they can model that with the base ten blocks? **Marcus:** I can. See, you count 120 and then 10 more you grab these. Now you have 130. **Teacher:** Ok. What about if Kiyana had 141 marbles and she got 10 more? **Mike:** You would count out 141 and then 10 more would be 151.

Introduction

Checking for Understanding	**Teacher:** Yes, and I just have a question . . . what does that word "equals" mean?
	Katie: Equals means the same as, so 141 plus 10 is the same as 151.
	The teacher reads two more problems that the group discusses.
	Teacher: What is the pattern? Who can describe what we see?
	Joe: We are changing the tens. So the number in the tens gets bigger by ten when we add 10.
	Teacher: Ok. I am going to give each one of you your own problem. I want you to read it. Solve it. Be ready to share how you did it. I am going to watch you and if you need help, look at our anchor charts and of course you can ask me.
	Teacher: How would we write and read that equation?
	Tom: 141 + 10 = 151.

Figure 8.24 Student Activity

	Student Activity
Guided Practice/ Checking for Understanding	The teacher passes out the problems. Students pull a card and act out their problems. The students each get a chance to share their problem and explain how they solved it. **Timmy:** Woooahh! My problem is this: $$\boxed{92 + 10}$$ **Timmy:** So I count out 92. . . and then add 10 more . . . 102! **Teacher:** Ok, what is the number sentence? **Timmy:** 92 + 10 is the same as 102. **Teacher:** What happened in this problem? **Lucy:** We had to get a hundred! **Teacher:** Why? **Mike:** Because we had 10 tens now and so we had to make a hundred.
Set Up for Independent Practice	*Every child shares out their problem and how they solved it.* **Teacher:** We are going to be talking more about this in the upcoming days. Are there any questions? What was interesting today? What was tricky?

Figure 8.25 Lesson Close

Close
♦ What did we do today? ♦ What was the math we were practicing? ♦ Was this easy or tricky? ♦ Turn to a partner and state one thing you learned today.

Figure 8.26 Add 10 Cards

180 + 10	109 + 10
139 + 10	143+ 10
120 + 10	100 + 10
150 + 10	190 + 10
175 + 10	Make up your own problem!

Figure 8.27 Challenge Version

10 + __ = 120	10 + __ = 130
__ + 10 = 135	___ + 10 = 150
__ + 10 = 160	10 + __ = 140
___ + 10 = 180	___+ 10 = 190
___ + 10 = 170	___+ 10 = ___

Pictorial Lesson

Figure 8.28 Pictorial Introduction

Introduction

Launch	**Teacher:** Today we are going to continue working on adding 10 to a number. We will be looking at how we can do that pictorially. **Vocabulary:** add, ten, sum, addend, plus, equals, makes **Math Talk:** _____ plus 10 is _____.
Model	**Teacher:** Notice what I have here. This is our hundred grid mat that we have worked with before. Today we are going to do shading to add tens. Look at my example. See, I shaded in 130 and then I shaded in 10 more. I have represented 130 + 10 to get a total of 140. I can say 130 plus 10 makes 140.
Checking for Understanding	**Teacher:** I am going to give each one of you an equation. I want you to practice representing it with your hundred grid mat. Then, you will explain what you did and what the equation is. Who wants to go first?

Figure 8.29 Student Activity

	Student Activity
Guided Practice/ Checking for Understanding	The teacher passes out cards with equations. Students pull a card and represent their thinking. The students each get a chance to share their problem and explain how they solved it. $\boxed{140 + 10}$ **Leslie:** I got 140 + 10. That makes 150. 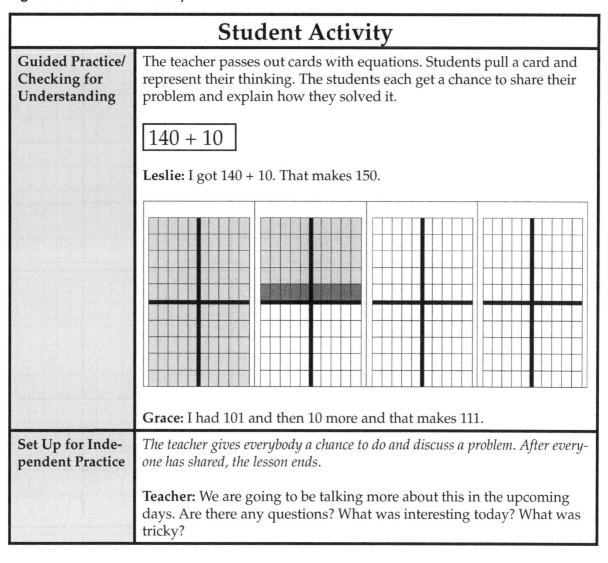 **Grace:** I had 101 and then 10 more and that makes 111.
Set Up for Independent Practice	*The teacher gives everybody a chance to do and discuss a problem. After everyone has shared, the lesson ends.* **Teacher:** We are going to be talking more about this in the upcoming days. Are there any questions? What was interesting today? What was tricky?

Figure 8.30 Lesson Close

Close
♦ What did we do today? ♦ What was the math we were practicing? ♦ Was this easy or tricky? ♦ Turn to a partner and state one thing you learned today.

Figure 8.31 Hundred Mat

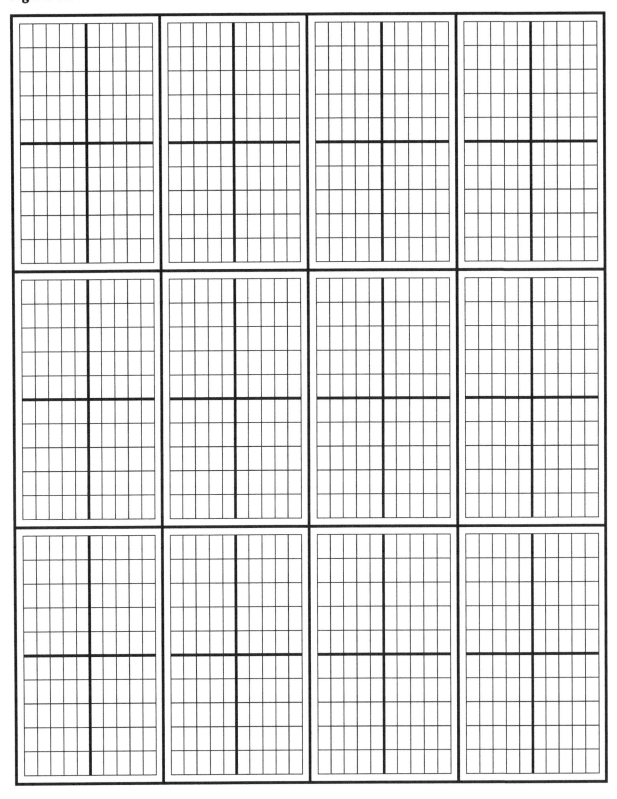

Abstract Lesson

Figure 8.32 Abstract Introduction

	Introduction
Launch	**Teacher:** Today we are going to continue working on adding 10 to a number. **Vocabulary:** add, ten, sum, addend, plus, equals, makes **Math Talk:** _____ plus 10 is _____.
Model	**Teacher:** Today we are going to continue to work on adding 10 by playing a game. I am going to teach you how to play Add 10 Concentration. This is a concentration game, and you all know how to play Concentration. But today you are going to be matching the "expression" with the "sum." Let me show you what that looks like. <table><tr><td>140 + 10</td><td>150</td><td>200</td><td>190 + 10</td></tr></table> So you will take turns trying to match the cards. Who can tell me how these cards should match up? **Ann:** 140 + 10 makes 150. **Chung:** 190 + 10 equals 200.
Checking for Understanding	**Teacher:** Yes, you got it. This is exactly what you are going to do. I am going to give you and your partner a set of cards and you will take turns looking for the matches. When all the cards are gone, whoever has the most pairs wins the game. When you are done, just mix them up and play again. If you get stuck, you can use your 300 grid.

Figure 8.33 Student Activity

Student Activity

Guided Practice/ Checking for Understanding	The teacher continues to watch the groups as they work on matching their problems. When everyone has finished the teacher asks the students to explain their thinking. She also asks them what was easy and what was tricky. Terri and Annie play the game. Each time they find a pair they have to state the equation. **Terri:** Oh, that's not a match. |	150		120 + 10
---|---|---|---| **Ann:** Yeah! I got a match. 175 plus 10 equals 185. | 175 + 10		185	
---	---	---	---	 *The students continue to play the game until they are done.*
Set Up for Independent Practice	*The teacher watches how the students are doing, who knows the answer right away, and who gets stuck. S/he is noticing who has to use their tools and who just knows it by heart.*

* Teacher Notes

David he is having some trouble . . . he uses the number hundred grid a lot	Annie she knows it
Marcus he knows it	Daniella she is counting on her fingers up ten each time

Figure 8.34 Lesson Close

Close

♦ What did we do today?
♦ What was the math we were practicing?
♦ Was this easy or tricky?
♦ Turn to a partner and state one thing you learned today.

Figure 8.35 Match Game Cards

$125 + 10$	$234 + 10$	$335 + 10$	$447 + 10$
$599 + 10$	$635 + 10$	$777 + 10$	$802 + 10$
$990 + 10$	$412 + 10$	135	244
345	457	609	645
787	812	1000	422

Section Summary

Adding 10 to a number gets tricky for students when it is a 3-digit number. Many times students will make 121 plus 10 into 221 instead of 131. All students should start with the concept pictorially and then sketch it out and connect it to the equation. Too often we jump to abstract practice, having students solve these only with equations, and so students stay shaky all year long. Which brings us to the next big idea, that this skill should be done as energizers, routines, and workstations throughout the year.

Figure 8.36 Overview

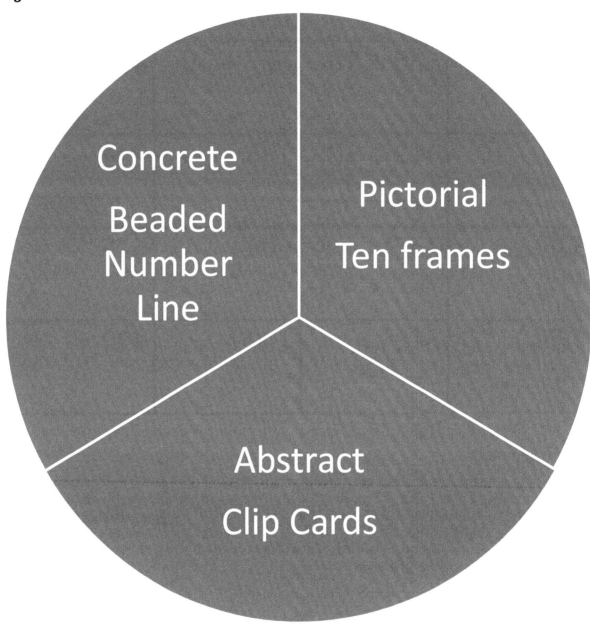

Figure 8.37 Planning Template

Adding Two 2-Digit Numbers

Big Idea: Using place value, you can add two numbers. **Enduring Understanding:** We can model problems in many ways. **Essential Question:** What are the ways to model the addition of two numbers? **I can statement:** I can model adding two numbers in different ways.	**Materials** ♦ Tools: Rekenrek ♦ Tools: Beaded Number Line ♦ Templates: Ten Frames ♦ Cards ♦ Crayons
Cycle of Engagement **Concrete:** Beaded Number Line  Sketch: 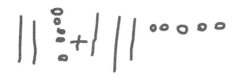 Abstract Equations: 25 + 35 20 + 5 + 30 + 5 = 50 + 10 = 60	**Vocabulary & Language Frames** ♦ Count back ♦ Difference _____ minus _____ makes ____.
	Pictorial: Drawing 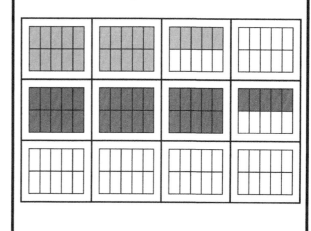

Figure 8.38 Differentiated Lessons

Three Differentiated Lessons		
In this series of lessons, students are working on the concept of *adding 2-digit numbers*. They are developing this concept through concrete activities, pictorial activities, and abstract activities. Here are some things to think about as you do these lessons.		
Emerging	**On Grade Level**	**Above Grade Level**
Do a lot of work with strategies. Use the beaded number line and the base ten blocks.	The standard is that students understand a variety of strategies.	Extend number range.
Looking for Misunderstandings and Common Errors		
Too often teachers rush students to the traditional algorithm. Be sure that everybody has two or three ways to think about adding numbers before you even start talking about the traditional algorithm. It is simply another way, not the focus of the grade. Students should work on adding tens and ones and finding friendly numbers at least.		

Figure 8.39 Anchor Chart

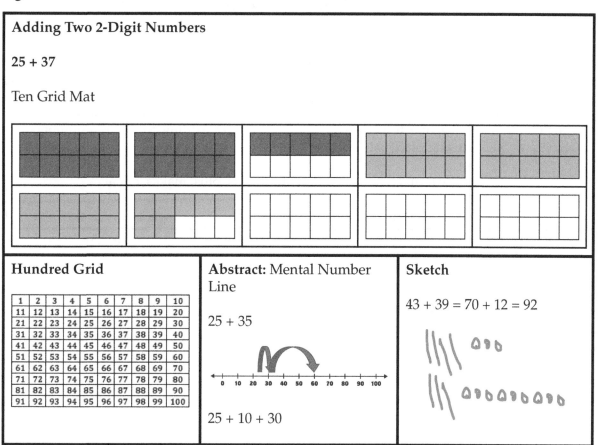

Adding Two 2-Digit Numbers		
25 + 37		
Ten Grid Mat		

Hundred Grid

1	2	3	4	5	6	7	8	9	10
11	12	13	14	15	16	17	18	19	20
21	22	23	24	25	26	27	28	29	30
31	32	33	34	35	36	37	38	39	40
41	42	43	44	45	46	47	48	49	50
51	52	53	54	55	56	57	58	59	60
61	62	63	64	65	66	67	68	69	70
71	72	73	74	75	76	77	78	79	80
81	82	83	84	85	86	87	88	89	90
91	92	93	94	95	96	97	98	99	100

Abstract: Mental Number Line

25 + 35

25 + 10 + 30

Sketch

43 + 39 = 70 + 12 = 92

Concrete Lesson

Figure 8.40 Concrete Introduction

	Introduction
Launch	**Teacher:** Today we are going to work on adding two 2-digit numbers using place value blocks. **Vocabulary:** add, addition, tens, ones, plus, makes, equals **Math Talk:** _____ plus_____ equals _____.
Model	**Teacher:** What if I had 34 marbles and I got 17 more? Who thinks they can model that? **Jason:** I can. See you can count 30 and 10 and then 7 and 4 more. I got 51. **Teacher:** That's a great way. Who has another way? **Cynthia:** It has a 7 so you could make 17 into a 20 by taking 3 from 34. Then, you would need to add 31 more. That makes 51.
Checking for Understanding	*The teacher reads two more problems that the group discusses.* **Teacher:** Ok. I am going to give each one of you your own problem. I want you to read it. Solve it. Be ready to share how you did it. I am going to watch you and if you need help, look at our anchor charts and of course you can ask me.

Figure 8.41 Student Activity

Student Activity	
Guided Practice/ Checking for Understanding	The teacher passes out the problems. Students pull a card and act out their problems. The students each get a chance to share their problem and explain how they solved it. **Timmy:** Woooahh! My problem is this: 59 + 28 **Timmy:** So I count out 59. . . And then I move 1 up to make another 10. So I have 60 and 27 left which is 87.
Set Up for Independent Practice	**Teacher:** Great. So what strategy did you use? I used "give and take." I took 1 from 28 and gave it to 59. I made an easier problem. *Every child shares out their problem and how they solved it on the beaded number line.* **Teacher:** We are going to be talking more about this in the upcoming days. Are there any questions? What was interesting today? What was tricky?

Figure 8.42 Lesson Close

Close
◆ What did we do today?   ◆ What was the math we were practicing?   ◆ Was this easy or tricky?   ◆ Turn to a partner and state one thing you learned today.

Figure 8.43 Adding 2-Digit Number Cards

81 + 19	44 + 38
32 + 47	26 + 67
25 + 59	19 + 72
58 + 26	67 +25
73+ 18	Make up your own problem!

Figure 8.44 Challenge Version

Add two numbers that have a sum of 50. They cannot be tens.	Add two numbers that almost make 70. They cannot be tens.
Add two numbers that make a little more than 90. They cannot be tens.	Add two numbers that have a sum of 82.
Add two numbers that make a little less than 40. They cannot be tens.	Add two numbers that have a sum of 55.
Add two numbers that make a little more than 75.	Add two numbers that make a little less than 100.
57 +? = 72	88 = 41 +?
? + 54 = 91	__ + __ = __

Pictorial Lesson

Figure 8.45 Pictorial Introduction

Introduction

Launch	**Teacher:** Today we are going to work on adding two 2-digit numbers using our beaded number line. **Vocabulary:** add, addition, tens, ones, plus, makes, equals **Math Talk:** ____ plus____ equals _____.
Model	**Teacher:** Today we are going to continue working on adding two 2-digit numbers. We will be looking at how we can do that pictorially with our ten frame mat. Notice what I have here. This is our ten frame hundred mat that we have worked with before. Today we are going to do shading to add numbers. Look at my example. See, I shaded in 28 and then I shaded 35. I could first add my tens. I have 20 + 30. Then I can add 8 and 5. . . first I can cover the 2 empty ones in the 8 to make a 10 and then I'll have 3 left so that is a total of 13. 50 and 13 equals 63.
Checking for Understanding	**Teacher:** I am going to give each one of you an equation. I want you to practice representing it with your ten frames. Then, you will explain what you did and what the equation is. Who wants to go first?

Figure 8.46 Student Activity

	Student Activity
Guided Practice/ Checking for Understanding	The teacher passes out cards with equations. Students pull a card and represent their thinking. The students each get a chance to share their problem and explain how they solved it. **Kelly:** I got $49 + 23$ So, I added my tens: 40 + 20 makes 60. Then I added 9 and 3 which is 12. So 60 and 12 make 72.
Set Up for Independent Practice	*The teacher gives everybody a chance to do and discuss a problem. After everyone has shared, the lesson ends.* **Teacher:** We are going to be talking more about this in the upcoming days. Are there any questions? What was interesting today? What was tricky?

Figure 8.47 Lesson Close

Close
◆ What did we do today? ◆ What was the math we were practicing? ◆ Was this easy or tricky? ◆ Turn to a partner and state one thing you learned today.

Figure 8.48 Ten Frame Shading Cards

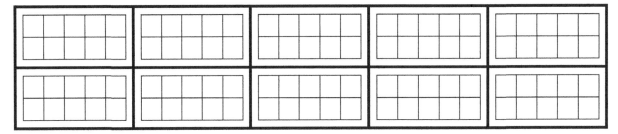

Figure 8.49 Expression Cards

85 + 19	44 + 36
37 + 47	28 + 64
25 + 55	19 + 78
58 + 23	67 + 29
79+ 12	Make up your own problem!

Abstract Lesson

Figure 8.50 Abstract Introduction

	Introduction
Launch	**Teacher:** Today we are going to work on adding two 2-digit numbers by just thinking about strategies. **Vocabulary:** add, addition, tens, ones, plus, makes, equals **Math Talk:** ____ plus____ equals _____.
Model	**Teacher:** Today we are going to continue to work on adding two 2-digit numbers. We are going to do it with our clip cards. Here is an example. You have to read the problem and then clip the correct answer with your clothespin. Then, when you are done, you check it by turning it over and seeing if the dot is where you clipped it. You just keep playing until you have done the whole pack. As you are doing it, sort them into piles of the ones you got right and the ones you got wrong. When you are finished, try the ones you got wrong over again. Let's look at this one. <table><tr><td colspan="3" align="center">34 + 57</td></tr><tr><td>71</td><td>81</td><td>91</td></tr></table> **Ann:** 30 + 50 equals 80 and then 7 and 4 is 11. 80 and 11 is 91. (*She pinches that number, then she flips it to check her answer.*)
Checking for Understanding	**Teacher:** Yes, you got it. This is exactly what you are going to do. I am going to give each of you your own set of cards. Also, here is a hundred grid if you want to use it to double-check your work.

Figure 8.51 Student Activity

	Student Activity
Guided Practice/ Checking for Understanding	The teacher continues to watch the groups as they work on matching their problems. When everyone has finished, the teacher asks the students to explain their thinking. She also asks them what was easy and what was tricky. **Katie:** <table><tr><td colspan="3" align="center">39 + 12</td></tr><tr><td>51</td><td>2</td><td>1</td></tr></table> It is 51. Let's see . . . I'm correct. **Teacher:** What strategy did you use? **Katie:** I made 39 a 40 and then added 11.
Set Up for Independent Practice	*The students continue to play the game until they are done. The teacher watches how the students are doing, who knows the answer right away, and who gets stuck. Who has to use their tools and who just knows it by heart.*

*Teacher Notes

Ted he can do it	Katie she can do it
Chung he is counting on his fingers	Lisa she uses the hundred grid

Figure 8.52 Lesson Close

Close
♦ What did we do today? ♦ What was the math we were practicing? ♦ What were we doing with our number wands? ♦ Was this easy or tricky? ♦ Turn to a partner and state one thing you learned today.

Figure 8.53 Clip Cards

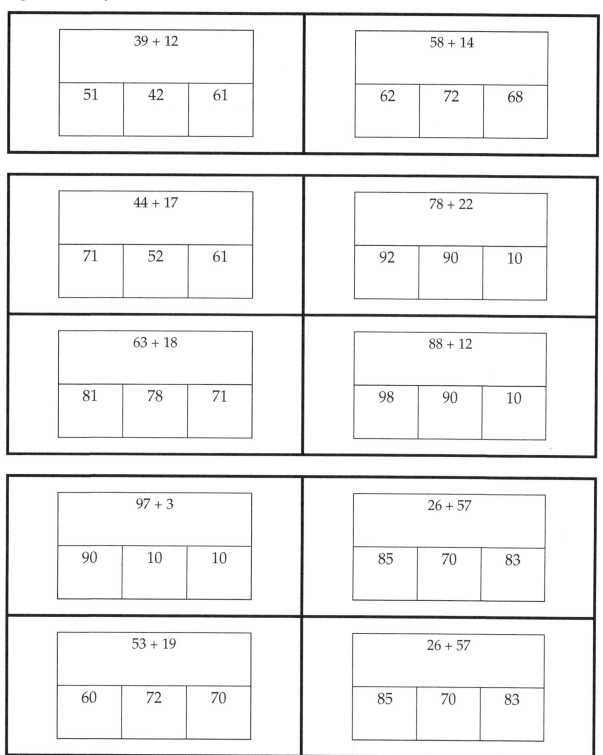

39 + 12		
51	42	61

58 + 14		
62	72	68

44 + 17		
71	52	61

78 + 22		
92	90	10

63 + 18		
81	78	71

88 + 12		
98	90	10

97 + 3		
90	10	10

26 + 57		
85	70	83

53 + 19		
60	72	70

26 + 57		
85	70	83

Section Summary

Adding 2-digit numbers is tricky. Students have a lot of difficulty when they are rushed to the algorithm. I find that place value blocks are one of the best ways to get students to see the strategies that we are teaching. I also like to use the beaded number line. For example, when you add 29 + 45, students can see that the 29 is right next to 30 so they understand when we say that we are going to make the 29 into a 30 and take one away from 45 and make it 44. Also, on the beaded number line you can get students to see how to add tens and ones very clearly. Eventually you move them from the beaded number line to a marked number line. Eventually they are ready to go to the open number line with understanding. Even with that, it works great if you lay down the place value blocks to show the jumps at first. The point is to practice in several different ways.

Figure 8.54 Overview

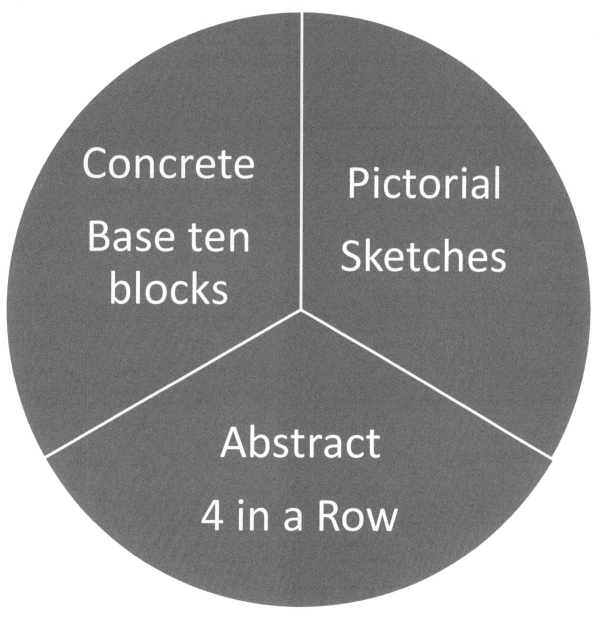

Figure 8.55 Planning Template

Comparing Numbers

Big Idea: Using place value you describe and compare numbers.

Enduring Understanding: We can compare numbers with words, models, and symbols.

Essential Question: What are the ways to compare numbers?

I can statement: I can compare numbers with words, models, and symbols.

Materials
- Tools: Beaded Number Line
- Templates: Ten Frame
- Cards
- Crayons

Cycle of Engagement

Concrete:

Pictorial: Drawing

Abstract: Hundred Grid

1	2	3	4	5	6	7	8	9	10
11	12	13	14	15	16	17	18	19	20
21	22	23	24	25	26	27	28	29	30
31	32	33	34	35	36	37	38	39	40
41	42	43	44	45	46	47	48	49	50
51	52	53	54	55	56	57	58	59	60
61	62	63	64	65	66	67	68	69	70
71	72	73	74	75	76	77	78	79	80
81	82	83	84	85	86	87	88	89	90
91	92	93	94	95	96	97	98	99	100

Vocabulary & Language Frames

- Tens, Ones, Hundreds
- Compare
- Greater than
- Less than
- Equal to

_____ is greater than_____.
_____ is less than_____.
_____ is the same as _____.

Figure 8.56 Differentiation

Three Differentiated Lessons		
In this series of lessons, students are working on the concept of *comparing numbers*. They are developing this concept through concrete activities, pictorial activities, and abstract activities. Here are some things to think about as you do these lessons.		
Emerging	**On Grade Level**	**Above Grade Level**
Do a lot of work with students comparing 2-digit numbers and then 3-digit umbers.	The grade-level standard is that students can compare 3-digit numbers.	Work with larger numbers.

Looking for Misunderstandings and Common Errors

Remember that the cycle for teaching comparing numbers is matching, counting, and then mental number line and reasoning about numbers.

Figure 8.57 Anchor Chart

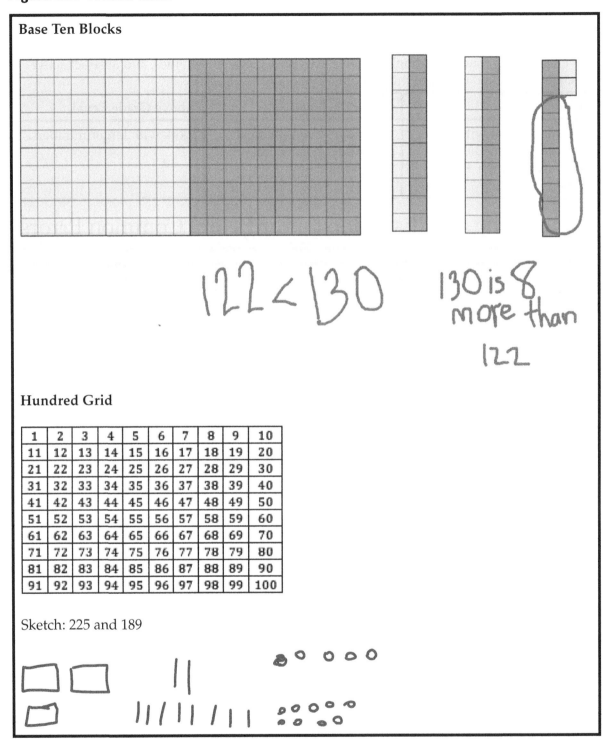

Base Ten Blocks

122 < 130

130 is 8 more than 122

Hundred Grid

1	2	3	4	5	6	7	8	9	10
11	12	13	14	15	16	17	18	19	20
21	22	23	24	25	26	27	28	29	30
31	32	33	34	35	36	37	38	39	40
41	42	43	44	45	46	47	48	49	50
51	52	53	54	55	56	57	58	59	60
61	62	63	64	65	66	67	68	69	70
71	72	73	74	75	76	77	78	79	80
81	82	83	84	85	86	87	88	89	90
91	92	93	94	95	96	97	98	99	100

Sketch: 225 and 189

Concrete Lesson

Figure 8.58 Concrete Introduction

	Introduction
Launch	**Teacher:** Today we are going to work on comparing numbers using words and tools. **Vocabulary:** greater than, less than, equal to, same as, tens, ones, hundreds **Math Talk:** _____ is greater than_____. _____ is less than_____. _____ is the same as _____.
Model	**Teacher:** Here are two numbers: 154 and 171. Who can compare them? **Carole:** I can. Ok, I am going to build it with the blocks. See, 171 is bigger. The hundreds are the same and the tens in 171 are more than the tens in 154. **Teacher:** What if Sue had 128 marbles and Lyle had 135? Who has more? How many more? **Marcus:** I can do it. See, here is 128 and here is 135. The hundreds are the same. There are 3 tens in 135 and only 2 tens in 128. Lyle has 7 more marbles than Sue. **Teacher:** So tell me about comparing numbers. What do you look for? **Kalie:** You have to compare the hundreds, then the tens, then the ones. The place that has the bigger number is the bigger number.
Checking for Understanding	_The teacher reads two more problems that the group discusses._ **Teacher:** Ok. I am going to give each one of you your own problem. I want you to read it. Solve it. Be ready to share how you did it. I am going to watch you and if you need help, look at our anchor charts and of course you can ask me.

Figure 8.59 Student Activity

	Student Activity
Guided Practice/ Checking for Understanding	The teacher passes out the problems. Students pull a card and act out their problems. The students each get a chance to share their problem and explain how they solved it. **Mia:** Woooahh! My numbers are: **Mia:** So I matched things. I matched the hundreds first. I have 2 hundreds in one number and 1 hundred in the other. So 205 is more than 109.
Set Up for Independent Practice	*Every child shares out their problem and how they solved it.* **Teacher:** We are going to be talking more about this in the upcoming days. Are there any questions? What was interesting today? What was tricky?

Figure 8.60 Lesson Close

Close
◆ What did we do today? ◆ What was the math we were practicing? ◆ Was this easy or tricky? ◆ Turn to a partner and state one thing you learned today.

Figure 8.61 Cards for Comparing Numbers

Compare 187 and 104	Compare 271 and 792
Compare 187 and 104	Compare 271 and 472
Compare 337 and 104	Compare 401 and 792
Compare 129 and 102	Compare 311 and 850
Compare 331 and 604	Compare 121 and 999
Compare 237 and 104	Compare 231 and 1092
Compare 107 and 110	Compare 941 and 555
Compare 125 and 104	Compare 201 and 702
Compare 134 and 154	Compare 299 and 400
Compare 356 and 144	Compare 435 and 777
Compare 131 and 132	Compare 357 and 859
Compare 307 and 624	Compare 100 and 990
Compare 207 and 114	Compare 1000 and 100
Compare 147 and 110	Compare 900 and 500

Pictorial Lesson

Figure 8.62 Pictorial Introduction

Introduction	
Launch	**Teacher:** Today we are going to continue working comparing two numbers with symbols. Here is a card with two numbers. Which symbol should we circle to make the statement true? Remember that the symbol opens towards the big number. Also, do a sketch to prove your thinking is correct. **Vocabulary:** greater than, less than, equal to, same as, tens, ones, hundreds **Math Talk:** _____ is greater than_____. _____ is less than_____. _____ is the same as _____.
Model	125 $<$ 159 ⃝ $=$ $>$ **Hong:** They both have hundreds. 25 is less than 59 because there are 5 tens in 59 and in 25 there are only 2 tens.
Checking for Understanding	**Teacher:** I am going to give each one of you an equation. I want you to practice representing it with your ten frames. Then, you will explain what you did and what the equation is. Who wants to go first?

Figure 8.63 Student Activity

Student Activity

Guided Practice/ Checking for Understanding	The teacher passes out cards with equations. Students pull a card and represent their thinking. The students each get a chance to share their problem and explain how they solved it. **Sean:** I got this problem. 129 is less than 130 because 30 is bigger than 29. They both have a hundred.
Set Up for Independent Practice	*The teacher gives everybody a chance to do and discuss a problem. After everyone has shared, the lesson ends.* **Teacher:** We are going to be talking more about this in the upcoming days. Are there any questions? What was interesting today? What was tricky?

Figure 8.64 Lesson Close

Close

♦ What did we do today?
♦ What was the math we were practicing?
♦ Was this easy or tricky?
♦ Turn to a partner and state one thing you learned today.

Figure 8.65 Compare Cards

425 < 193 = >	290 < 330 = >
529 < 530 = >	511 < 808 = >
129 < 230 = >	123 < 379 = >
429 < 530 = >	508 < 499 = >
709 < 808 = >	900 < 1030 = >
607 < 599 = >	1029 < 1290 = >

Abstract Lesson

Figure 8.66 Abstract Introduction

<table>
<tr><td colspan="2" align="center"><h2>Introduction</h2></td></tr>
<tr>
<td>Launch</td>
<td>

Teacher: Today we are going to play four in a row. You and your partner pull a card.

Vocabulary: greater than, less than, equal to, same as, tens, ones, hundreds

Math Talk:
_____ is greater than_____.
_____ is less than_____.
_____ is the same as _____.

</td>
</tr>
<tr>
<td>Model</td>
<td></td>
</tr>
</table>

Monkeying around with numbers: Pull a card and cover a number that matches what it says. Whoever gets four in a row wins. Each partner uses a different color of counters.

154	253	388	490	577
1084	922	801	705	689
106	610	742	607	350
200	321	555	920	1012
999	800	435	899	775

cover a number greater than 500	cover a number greater than 200	cover a number greater than 300	cover a number greater than 900	cover a number greater than 100
cover a number less than 500	cover a number less than 100	cover a number less than 200	cover a number less than 900	cover a number less than 700
cover a number in between 200 and 500	cover a number in between 100 and 200	cover a number in between 400 and 600	cover a number in between 300 and 500	cover a number in between 500 and 700
cover a number in between 700 and 850	cover a number in between 800 and 900	cover a number in between 900 and 1200	cover a number in between 650 and 800	cover a number in between 450 and 550

Checking for Understanding	**Teacher:** Who can explain how to play?
	Tami: It's a four in a row game.
	Yasmin: You have to pull a card and follow the directions. Like if it says cover up a number greater than 300 then you have to do that.
	Teacher: Ok, any questions? Let's start.

Figure 8.67 Student Activity

Student Activity	
Guided Practice/ Checking for Understanding	**Kate:** I pulled a card that said cover a number greater than 500. So, I covered 922. **Luke:** I pulled a card that said cover a number less than 700 so I covered 435.

Place Value Cover Up! Play rock, paper, scissors to see who starts. Then, take turns pulling a card and covering a number that matches what it says. Each player uses a different color set of markers. Whoever gets four in a row first wins.

154	253	388	490	577
1084	922	801	705	689
106	610	742	607	350
200	321	555	920	1012
999	800	435	899	775

cover a number greater than 500	cover a number greater than 200	cover a number greater than 300	cover a number greater than 900	cover a number greater than 100
cover a number less than 500	cover a number less than 100	cover a number less than 200	cover a number less than 900	cover a number less than 700
cover a number in between 200 and 500	cover a number in between 100 and 200	cover a number in between 400 and 600	cover a number in between 300 and 500	cover a number in between 500 and 700
cover a number in between 700 and 850	cover a number in between 800 and 900	cover a number in between 900 and 1200	cover a number in between 650 and 800	cover a number in between 450 and 550

Set Up for Independent Practice	**Teacher:** Ok, you all will play this game in your workstations so you can practice place value.

Figure 8.68 Close

Close
◆ What did we do today?
◆ What was the math we were practicing?
◆ Was this easy or tricky?
◆ Turn to a partner and state one thing you learned today.

Figure 8.69

Four in a Row Game

Monkeying around with numbers: Pull a card and cover a number that matches what it says. Each player uses a different set of color markers. Whoever gets four in a row wins.

154	253	388	490	577
1084	922	801	705	689
106	610	742	607	350
200	321	555	920	1012
999	800	435	899	775

cover a number greater than 500	cover a number greater than 200	cover a number greater than 300	cover a number greater than 900	cover a number greater than 100
cover a number less than 500	cover a number less than 100	cover a number less than 200	cover a number less than 900	cover a number less than 700
cover a number in between 200 and 500	cover a number in between 100 and 200	cover a number in between 400 and 600	cover a number in between 300 and 500	cover a number in between 500 and 700
cover a number in between 700 and 850	cover a number in between 800 and 900	cover a number in between 900 and 1200	cover a number in between 650 and 800	cover a number in between 450 and 550

Section Summary

Comparing 3-digit numbers takes time. Oftentimes, people rush through the concrete part of teaching comparing numbers. Students should use the base ten blocks and actually match them up to see what has more and what has less and how much more and less. This is important because it allows students to talk very concretely about what they are doing and then eventually they can start drawing out those discussions. They should use their mathematical sketches to explain their thinking around comparing the numbers. After a while, bring in hundred grids and number lines, which eventually turn into the mental number line.

Depth of Knowledge

Depth of Knowledge (Figure 8.70) is a framework that encourages us to ask questions that require that students think, reason, explain, defend, and justify their thinking (Webb, 2002). Figure 8.71 is snapshot of what that can look like in terms of place value work.

Figure 8.70 DOK Activities

	What are different strategies and models that we can use to teach place and value?	What are different strategies and models that we can use to compare two numbers?	What are different strategies and models that we can use to model adding two numbers?
DOK Level 1 (These are questions where students are required to simply recall/reproduce an answer/do a procedure.)	How many hundreds, tens, and ones are in this number?	What number is greater than 235?	What is 23 + 58?
DOK Level 2 (These are questions where students have to use information, think about concepts and reason.) This is considered a more challenging problem than a level 1 problem.	Can you model the number 131 in two different ways?	Name a number that is greater than 227 and less than 344. Explain why your number is correct.	Can you model 23 + 58 in two different ways?
DOK Level 3 (These are questions where students have to reason, plan, explain, justify, and defend their thinking.)	Circle the ones that are not true and explain why. . . 200 + 11 = 211 100 + 111 = 211 20 tens plus 11 ones = 211 1 hundred, 10 tens, and 1 one = 211 20 tens + 11 tens = 211	Name a number that is greater than 255 and less than 361. Prove that your number is correct with numbers, words, and pictures.	___ + ___ = 81

Adapted from Kaplinsky (https://robertkaplinsky.com/depth-knowledge-matrix-elementary-math/). A great resource for asking open questions is Marion Small's *Good Questions: Great*

Ways to Differentiate Mathematics Instruction in the Standards-Based Classroom (2017). Kentucky Math Department (2007) has these great math matrices as well.

Figure 8.71 Asking rigorous questions:

DOK 1	DOK 2 **At this level, students explain their thinking.**	DOK 3 **At this level, students have to justify, defend, and prove their thinking with objects, drawings, and diagrams.**
What is the answer to. . . ? Can you model the number? Can you model the problem? Can you identify the answer that matches this equation? How many hundreds, tens, and ones are in this number?	How do you know that the equation is correct? Can you pick the correct answer and explain why it is correct? How can you model that problem? What is another way to model that problem? Can you model that on the. . . ? Give me an example of a . . . type of problem. . . Which answer is incorrect? Explain your thinking.	Can you prove that your answer is correct? Prove that. . . Explain why that is the answer. . . . Show me how to solve that and explain what you are doing. Defend your thinking.

Key Points

- ◆ Concrete, Pictorial, and Abstract
- ◆ Composing and Decomposing Numbers
- ◆ Expanding Numbers
- ◆ Adding 10 to a Number
- ◆ Adding 2 and 3-Digit Numbers
- ◆ Comparing Numbers

Summary

It is important to spend time developing place value throughout the year. At the beginning of the year, be sure to spend a bit of time reviewing the place value standards from the year before through energizers and routines. During the first week of school, set up workstations to review the priority place value standards from the year before. Keep those workstations up all year and add the new ones as they are taught. Also, make sure that parents understand what the place value standards are and ways that they can help to develop it.

Reflection Questions

1. How are you currently teaching place value lessons?
2. Are you making sure that you do concrete, pictorial, and abstract activities?
3. What do your students struggle with the most and what ideas are you taking away from this chapter that might inform your work around those struggles?

References

Hanich, L. B., Jordan, N. C., Kaplan, D., & Dick, J. (2001). Performance across different areas of mathematical cognition in children with learning difficulties. *Journal of Educational Psychology, 93*, 615–626.

Jordan, N. C., & Hanich, L. B. (2000). Mathematical thinking in second-grade children with different forms of LD. *Journal of Learning Disabilities, 33*, 567–578.

Kamii, C. (1985). *Young children reinvent arithmetic*. New York, NY: Teachers College Press.

Kamii, C., & Joseph, L. (1988, Feburary). Teaching place value and two-column addition. *Arithmetic Teacher, 35*(6), 48–52.

Kentucky Department of Education (2007). Support Materials for Core Content for Assessment Version 4.1 Mathematics. Retrieved from the internet on January 15th, 2017.

Miura, I., Okamoto, Y., Chungsoon, K., & Steere, M. (1993). First graders' cognitive representations of understanding of place value: Cross-national comparisons-France, Japan, Korea, Sweden, and the United States. *Journal of Educational Psychology, 85*(1), 24–30.

Moeller, K., Pixner, S., Zuber, J., Kaufmann, L., & Nuerk, H. C. (2011). Early place-value understanding as a precursor for later arithmetic performance—a longitudinal study on numerical development. *Research in Developmental Disabilities, 32*(5), 1837–1851.

National Council of Teachers of Mathematics (NCTM). (2000). *Principles and standards for school mathematics*. Reston, VA: Author.

Sherman, H. J., Richardson, L. I., & Yard, G. J. (2013). *Teaching learners who struggle with mathematics: Systematic intervention and remediation*. Boston: Pearson.

Smalls, M. (2017). *Good questions: Great ways to differentiate mathematics instructions* (3rd ed.). New York, NY: TC Press.

Webb, N. (2002). *An analysis of the alignment between mathematics standards and assessments for three states*. Paper presented at the annual meeting of the American educational Research Association, New Orleans, LA.

9

Action Planning and FAQs

Well, to get started, you must get started. So pick where you want to start and just begin. Begin small. Here is an Action Checklist (see Figure 9.1):

Figure 9.1 Action Checklist

Before the Lesson	
Decide on the topic that you want to do.	
Why are you doing this topic?	
Is this emerging, on grade level, or advanced?	
Map out a 3-cycle connected lesson plan.	
What are you going to do concretely?	
What are you going to do pictorially?	
What are you going to do abstractly?	
What misconceptions and error patterns do you anticipate?	
During the Lessons	
What are your questions?	
How are the students doing?	
What do you notice?	
What do you hear?	
What do you see?	
After the Lessons	
What went well?	
What will you tweak?	
What will you do the same?	
What will you do differently?	

Before the Lesson	
What made you say "Wow!"	
What made you think "Uh-oh . . ."	
What did you notice?	
What did you wonder?	
Other Comments	

Frequently Asked Questions

1. **What Is a Guided Math Group?**
    Guided math is a temporary small group of students pulled out for instruction around a specific topic. Sometimes the groups are heterogeneous and sometimes they are homogeneous. It depends what you are teaching. If you are teaching a specific skill, like adding within 10, and you have some students who know it and others who are struggling, then you would pull the students who need to learn it into a small group. However, sometimes you are working on general concepts, like solving word problem with models. You can pull a heterogeneous group to teach this.

2. **Why Do Guided Math?**
    You do guided math for a variety of reasons. Lillian Katz (2019) said it best:

    > When a teacher tries to teach something to the entire class at the same time, chances are, one-third of the kids already know it; one-third will get it; and the remaining third won't. So two-thirds of the children are wasting their time.

    You do guided math so that everyone gets to learn. You can pull students for remedial work, on grade-level work, and enrichment. You do guided math so that students understand the math they are doing. You work with students in small groups so that they can talk, understand, reason, and do math!

3. **What Are the Types of Lessons?**
    There are five different types of guided math lessons. Conceptual, procedural, reasoning, strategy, and disposition. Disposition lessons are mostly integrated throughout the other lessons, but sometimes you just pull students and talk about their journey. That could look like, *what is tricky about what we are learning?* And, *what is easy?*

4. **Do You Always Use Manipulatives in a Guided Math Group?**
    No. It depends where you are in the cycle of developing the concepts and student understanding. You certainly should use manipulatives in the beginning when you are developing concepts, but eventually when students are practicing at the abstract level, they probably won't be working directly with manipulatives. Although, sometimes they still use them to check their answers or even solve problems if they need to.

5. **What About Doing Worksheets in Guided Math Groups?**
   Never. It's simple. Guided math is students doing math, not doing a worksheet. Sometimes, you do pull students to work on some specific problems on a journal page, but that is not the norm or the regular structure of a guided math group.

Reference

Katz, L. (2019). Retrieved April 15, 2019, from www.azquotes.com/author/39264-Lilian_Katz

For Product Safety Concerns and Information please contact our EU
representative GPSR@taylorandfrancis.com Taylor & Francis Verlag GmbH,
Kaufingerstraße 24, 80331 München, Germany

Printed and bound by CPI Group (UK) Ltd, Croydon, CR0 4YY
11/04/2025
01843980-0004